The Art of Benin

Paula Ben-Amos

THAMES AND HUDSON

© John Calmann & Cooper Ltd., 1980
This book was designed and produced by
John Calmann & Cooper Ltd., London

Filmset by Southern Positives and Negatives (SPAN), Lingfield, Surrey
Printed in Hong Kong by Mandarin Offset International Ltd

Library of Congress Catalog card number: 80–50794

Contents

Introduction

The art of the Benin Kingdom first came to the attention of the West in 1897 when members of a British naval expedition brought out thousands of objects as war booty. Through government and private sales, Benin sculpture soon found its way into museum and personal collections in England, Europe, and America. The British conquest of Benin resulted not only in the dispersal of the art, but it also wrought considerable changes in the fabric of Benin life. Once an independent warrior kingdom, Benin was now incorporated into the wider political framework of the British Protectorate of Nigeria and later the modern Nigerian state. Today Benin City, a thriving metropolis of over 160,000 people,[1] is the capital of the Bendel State of Nigeria.

What was the Benin Kingdom like before 1897? As yet we know little of its origins. Benin is located on a rolling coastal plain in an area of tropical rain forest. There is little in its geographical position to explain its development, for the lateritic soil and thick forest growth would not appear to facilitate agricultural production or trade and communications. Nevertheless, by the thirteenth or fourteenth centuries A.D. – or so oral traditions and archaeological investigations would seem to indicate – a state had emerged out of the numerous small clans and petty chiefdoms in the area.[2] By the fifteenth century it was an expanding warrior kingdom, as we learn from this account by Duarte Pacheco Pereira, a Portuguese explorer who visited Benin in the 1490s. In his work *Esmeraldo de Situ Orbis*, he describes Benin:

> The Kingdom of Beny is about eighty leagues long and forty wide; it is usually at war with its neighbours and takes many captives, whom we buy at twelve or fifteen brass bracelets each, or for copper bracelets which they prize more.[3]

The Portuguese, who were exploring the west coast of Africa in search of trade and converts, reached this area in the third quarter of the fifteenth century. 'Beny' or Benin, the name by which they knew it, is still used by us today, although the people call themselves, their language, their capital city, and their kingdom Edo.

From at least the fifteenth century the core of Benin political, religious, and social life was the divine kingship. The monarch or oba ruled by virtue of his descent from Oranmiyan, the legendary founder of the present dynasty. According to royal tradition, Oranmiyan was a Yoruba prince from the kingdom of Ife who came at the invitation of Benin elders dissatisfied with their previous rulers, the *Ogiso*. Like similar traditions among neighbouring Nigerian groups, this story of external origin of the ruler sets him apart from the ruled, a separateness reflected in his immense religious and political power.[4]

The religious basis of the Benin monarchy was noted by the earliest European visitors. In an account written about 1540 (published in

1. Brass altar of the Hand made for an eighteenth-century king. *18in (47·5cm). London, British Museum*

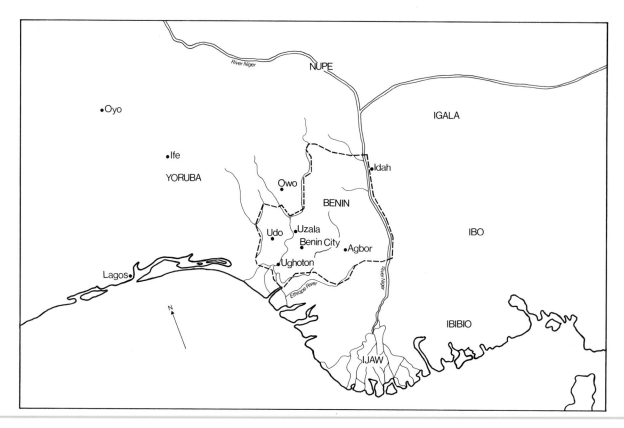

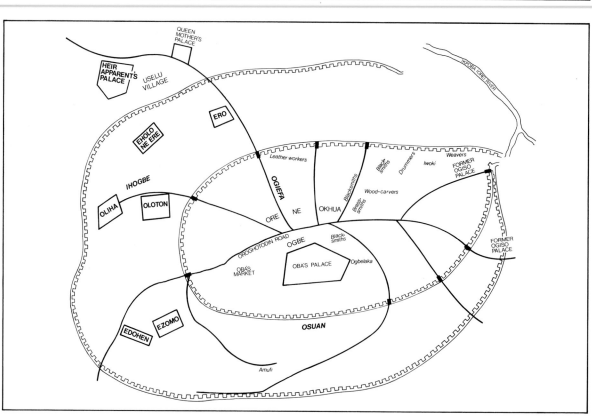

Map showing the kingdom of Benin.

G. B. Ramusio's *Navigazioni e Viaggi*, 1550), a Portuguese pilot portrayed divine kingship in Benin and neighbouring monarchies on the coast:

> The kings are worshipped by their subjects, who believe that they come from heaven, and speak of them always with great reverence, at a distance and on bended knees. Great ceremony surrounds them, and many of these kings never allow themselves to be seen eating, so as not to destroy the belief of their subjects that they can live without food.[5]

The oba's political powers were extensive: he was the last resort in court matters and dispenser of the death penalty, the recipient of taxes and tribute, the controller of trade, the titular owner of all the land in the kingdom, and the chief executive and legislator. Throughout Benin history there were, of course, both weak and strong obas, but however much the effective political power of the ruler waxed and waned, the ideology of divine kingship remained central to Benin political life.

The oba's senior son was in theory his rightful heir, at least during the last two hundred years. Since, however, the king had many wives it often occurred that more than one gave birth at the same time, and thus it was difficult to determine which son really was the most senior. For this reason, the brothers of an established oba – obviously potential rivals – were sent out to the countryside as hereditary rulers (*enogie*) over administrative districts. The mother of the king was given the title of Queen Mother and was set up in her own palace in the village of Uselu just outside the city.

The king lived in a vast palatial compound covering several acres of land. This complex included meeting chambers for various groups of chiefs, storehouses, shrine compounds, work areas for ritual specialists and royal craftsmen, and a residential section for the oba's numerous wives and small children. The Edo say, 'In the oba's palace there is never silence', an adage which expresses well the hustle and bustle of activities carried on there by a multitude of officials, servants, family members and chiefs.

The titled chiefs, together with the royal family, constituted the political elite of the kingdom. The highest ranking among the chiefs were the Seven Uzama, who were considered to be the descendants of the very elders of Benin who sent to Ife for Oranmiyan. As 'guardians of Benin custom', they had important roles to play in the installation of new kings and the annual worship of the departed ones. The other title holders – of which there were many – were broadly divided into Palace Chiefs, who lived in *Ogbe*, the king's sector of the city, and Town Chiefs, who lived across the main avenue in *Ore ne Okhua* (see left). The Palace Chiefs were a kind of old aristocracy, made up of

Map of Benin City showing the positions of the guilds and chiefs' houses.

3. Decorated shrine of Ogan, the local deity of Ekhua Village

members of 'good' urban families. They were concerned with the administration of the palace and belonged to one of three important palace associations: *Iwebo*, who cared for the oba's regalia, supervised his craftsmen, and conducted affairs with European traders visiting Benin; *Ibiwe*, who were in charge of caring for the oba's wives and children; and *Iweguae*, who provided the oba's domestic staff of officials, cooks, servants, and pages.

In contrast to the Palace Chiefs, the Town Chiefs tended to be the *nouveaux riches* who rose to power by their own efforts, not through inherited wealth and connections. They were responsible for the administration of the various territories of the kingdom, including the collection of tribute, the conscription of soldiers, and the mediation between royal and village interests.[6]

In the same area as the Town Chiefs lived numerous minor palace officials, chiefly retainers, and members of guilds, of which there were about forty or fifty. Each guild was located in a special ward and had a specific service to perform for the king. Their duties were indeed diverse, ranging from leopard hunters (plate 6) to drummers, executioners, astrologers, and land purifiers. Among these guilds were the craftsmen who produced brass, ivory, and wood sculpture, embroidered cloths, and leather fans for the oba and, with his permission, for the chiefs and cult priests in the city and throughout the kingdom.

These craftsmen constituted a kind of artisan class, for they lived in wards clustered in the same area and preferred their children to marry

2. The late King Akenzua II at the annual festival honouring his ancestors

4. Parlour floor in the house of the late Chief Ajayi-Oba. One of the special forms of decoration in a chief's house used to be embedding the parlour floor with cowrie shells, an earlier form of currency

5. A traditional chief's house, probably photographed in 1897. Architecture is one way of marking elite status in Benin. Chiefs own large compounds, the exterior walls of which are decorated with horizontal ridge designs (*agben*). Formerly, clay bas-relief designs of animals and warriors were an important part of architectural decoration but today this is rarely found. (*Photo: R. K. Granville*). *Oxford, Pitt Rivers Museum*

those of other craftsmen. They were all considered 'servants of the oba', that is his special dependants. The Edo adage 'Smiths and woodworkers will never suffer from poverty' expresses this continued economic support.

Outside of the capital the population was settled in villages, some with only a few hundred people, others perhaps with several thousand. In the past some attained the status of towns or even small city states: for example, the name of the town Urhonigbe, meaning 'ten gates', a gesture of bravado at Benin City which had only nine. Although these villages were mainly agricultural, some did specialize in crafts, such as the pottery centres of Oka, Use, and Utekon, or the carpenters of Idunmwun-Owina.

With a few exceptions, such as the carpenters mentioned above or the forgers of iron ceremonial swords from Igueban, village craftsmen were not 'servants of the king', as were their urban counterparts. They worked instead for their own communities, carving masks for village cult rituals and moulding life-size mud sculptures for local shrines. Creators of religious art, called *omebo* (literally 'moulder of the gods'), were chosen by divine inspiration and often acquired reputations over a wide area of the kingdom (plates 43 and 44).

The brasses, ivories, and other creations by the guild craftsmen – and to a lesser extent the wood, ceramic, and mud sculpture from the villages – have attracted much attention in the eighty or so years since Benin art was brought to the West. Indeed, a considerable body of scholarship has accumulated to which the reader can easily turn to find discussions about the origins and stylistic development of Benin art and its relation to other Nigerian artistic traditions.[7] The aim of this book is to provide a broad perspective on Benin art in its historical and cultural context based in large measure on materials gathered in the

6. (*Right*) Plaque of members of leopard hunters' guild, probably dating from the sixteenth century. The leopard is considered the king of all the creatures in the bush and is thus a counterpart of the oba, the king of the home or settled land. The killing of the leopard was a royal prerogative exercised only for ritual purposes. Members of the guild captured wild leopards and kept them for royal sacrifice. They also had charms to tame leopards so that the king could parade in the city with them, a sign of his domination over the king of the bush (see plate 20). *Height: 17in (43cm). London, British Museum.*

7. (*Far right*) Traditional oil lamp made by the blacksmith's guild. *Diameter: 14½in (36·5cm). Chicago, Field Museum of Natural History*

8. *(Below)* **Board for traditional game called** *ise.* **Guild carvers made not only religious items but objects for entertainment and household use. The guilloche pattern, called 'the rope of the world'** *(oba ne iri agbon)* **is common in Benin art as a mark of status.**
London, Courtesy Sotheby's

course of field research. The starting point is the Edo view of the history and meaning of their art. In a society as complex as Benin there are many different oral traditions about art, some of general currency, others held within special groups such as craft guilds. These traditions, when compared with European visitors' accounts and archaeological and ethnographic reports, can provide a temporal framework for understanding the broad historical context in which Benin art was created. In a like manner, the meaning of Benin art forms can be found in the proverbs, tales and artistic commentaries of the Edo themselves as well as in the description and analysis of the various contexts – domestic as well as royal, rural as well as urban – in which these forms are used.

It is not possible to cover fully the complexity of traditional art in Benin; this book can only be a beginning. The people of Benin are well aware of the complexity of their culture and have a proverb that can serve as a reminder to us all:

A gha se Edo, Edo rre

The closer one gets to Benin, the farther away it is.

Art, History and Politics

9. Brocaded cotton waist pennant. Weaving is thought to have originated in the Ogiso period. The guild, however, was not organized until the time of Oba Ohen, the eighth king in the new dynasty, who may have reigned in the early fifteenth century. Struck by paralysis, the oba was forced to cover his legs with cloth and therefore formed a guild for its provision. One of their first creations is said to be this type of waist pennant (*egbele*), worn by chiefs at ceremonies. 11¾in (30cm). Vienna, Museum für Völkerkunde

The Edo are profoundly concerned with their past achievements, which they preserve not in written records but in oral traditions. Among these are lists of kings and detailed accounts of their wars, adventures, and artistic innovations. The lists of kings provide a general historical framework, even though we do not know the exact dates of most of their reigns; the stories about their activities give us clues to the events of their times. As a result of European contact with Benin we have for the last four to five hundred years a remarkable collection of trade records, correspondence, and most especially, descriptions of Benin court life, customs, and art. Using all these materials it is possible to sketch the broad outline of Benin artistic and cultural history. Obviously such a picture is much more reliable as we get closer to the present. For the remote past, we can only speculate on developments, relying on oral history and the preliminary results of archaeology.

The Ogiso Period and Early Benin Art

The Edo view of their past is decidedly monarchical. From the very beginning Benin was ruled by a series of kings who were called *Ogiso*, or 'rulers of the sky'. Depending on the tradition, this dynasty consisted of thirty-one, twelve, or just one king.[8] A revolt by the Edo removed the *Ogiso* from the throne. After a brief attempt at republican government the Edo asked the King of Ife in Yorubaland for one of his sons to rule them. He sent Oranmiyan, whose own son Eweka became the first oba in the dynasty which rules Benin today. By estimating the average reigns of obas, scholars have suggested that the new dynasty was founded in the fourteenth century or somewhat earlier. The transition to this new dynasty symbolizes a change in fundamental temporal and spatial orientation. The *Ogiso* period is archaic and essentially mythological. Neither strict chronology nor the exact number of kings is important. The second dynasty, in contrast, is founded on temporal duration and the activities, personalities, and innovations of nearly every oba are remembered in lavish detail.[9]

The establishment of a Yoruba dynasty brought Benin into a wider political and cultural orbit and redirected its spatial orientation from east to west. The east is the cardinal direction associated with the creator god, Osanobua, and with the creation of the land, which first rose out of the primordial waters in a place which today is the Igbo town of Agbor to the east of Benin. All the sites where once the *Ogisos* built their palaces and ancient quarters are on the eastern side of the present city. In contrast, the founder of the second dynasty came from Yorubaland, to the west of Edo, and many of the important early obas came from western districts of the Benin kingdom. The change in spatial orientation was accompanied by a shift from a closed society to

an open one; Benin became cosmopolitan, receptive to foreign ideas not only from the Yoruba but, through expansion and trade, from other neighbouring groups and eventually from the Western world.

The arts and crafts associated with the *Ogiso* period are those considered most basic for survival and closest to the core of Benin social, political, and religious life. These include domestic implements, such as wooden kitchen utensils and iron tools, as well as woven raffia cloth and leather ceremonial boxes (plates 90 and 91).[10] Jewellery made of brass was worn as adornment. According to the traditional song:

> Evikurure, the daughter of *Ogiso*,
> When she raises her hand, brass sounds *giengheren**
> When she raises her leg, brass sounds *giengheren*

Art forms crucial to status differentiation and religious worship are attributed to *Ogiso* times, particularly the rectangular throne (*agba*), the ceremonial sword (*ada*), and the ancestral commemorative head

*(*giengheren* is an onomatopaeic word for jingling)

10. Wooden stool (*agba*). With the transition from the Ogiso dynasty to the Oranmiyan one, the *agba* was superseded by the round throne (*ekete*) which has strong Yoruba associations. Today the king uses an *agba* for non-ceremonial purposes and the chiefs own them as marks of their high status. While the Edo view the *agba* as one of their oldest types of stools, the rectangular form and additive construction are not common in sub-Saharan Africa and may be derived from a European prototype.[11] *Height: 17¼in (44cm). Philadelphia, University of Pennsylvania Museum*

11. A ceremonial sword (*ada*) with an iron blade and brass leopard decorations. The *ada* is carried by pages (*emada*) during the public appearances of the oba. It symbolizes his right to take human life. The oba delegates the *ada* to high-ranking chiefs who may have it carried alongside them in their own domains but not in the palace. *38in (96cm). Copenhagen, National Museum of Denmark (Dept. of Ethnography)*

(*uhunmwun-elao*). It is interesting that in the traditions surrounding these objects, each undergoes a transformation with the arrival of the new dynasty. Oral history indicates that the political transition was not without conflict and, as we shall see, stories about these three objects clearly reflect the struggles of the new kings to consolidate their rule over the Edo people.

The *agba* (plate 10) is an elaborately carved stool which once served as the throne of the *Ogiso* kings. Its political importance is embedded in the language: the Edo phrase for convening a meeting means literally to 'bring out an *agba*'. Possession of the *agba* was in early times the mark of legitimate authority. In his difficult struggle against representatives of the former regime, the fourth oba, Ewedo, finally wrested the stool of the *Ogiso* from them and thus established his authority in Benin.[12]

In *Ogiso* times the iron ceremonial sword called *ada* (plate 11) was part of the furnishings of the ancestral altar, where it expressed the power of the ancestors to control the course of events. The Edo believe that iron has the mystical power of *ase* to insure that whatever proclamations are made will come to pass. In the second dynasty, the obas took to making public appearances accompanied by pages carrying the *ada*, thereby incorporating an ancient Edo sanction into the new royal symbolism.

Ancestral commemorative heads, *uhunmwun-elao*, have existed since earliest times as a way of honouring the deceased and beautifying ancestral shrines. They were made of different materials, depending on the political and occupational status of the owner. Sculptures of wood for chiefly altars originated either in the *Ogiso* period, as royal traditions would have it,[13] or well into the new dynasty, according to members of the carvers' guild (plate 66). Terracottas – today found only in the ward of brass-casters – were formerly the most widespread commemorative sculpture, used on the royal ancestral altars of the *Ogiso* kings and on shrines in Idunmwun Ivbioto, the quarter of the 'sons of the soil', built in *Ogiso* times, and in Idunmwun Ogiefa, the ward guild responsible for purifying the land after the violation of taboos. Breaking away from this association with ancestral soil and early rulers, the obas of the second dynasty introduced the brass commemorative head as their own distinctive shrine decoration (plate 39). The significance of brass, at least in the modern Edo view, derives from its red colour and shiny surface, qualities which are considered both beautiful and frightening – a particularly appropriate symbol for the monarchy.

The question of the origin of brass-casting in Benin is intriguing and far from being resolved. For over fifty years there have been attempts by colonial officials, historians, and anthropologists to

12. Terracotta commemorative head. There are nearly sixty of these heads in museums and private collections, over half of which have holes in the crown.[16] **Chief Ihama of the brass-smiths claims the holes were for the insertion of ivory tusks and that the terracotta heads were used by the** *Ogiso* **rulers on their paternal ancestral altars, much as the obas use ivory tusks on brass heads (plate 68). The ancient practice of sending younger brothers of the ruler, who were potential rivals for the throne, to govern rural areas means that terracotta heads associated with the** *Ogiso* **dynasty might still be found in villages dating from that period.** *Zurich, Museum Rietburg*

13. Terracotta head on a village age-grade promotion shrine in the Isi District. Terracotta sculpture has been coming to light in the last twenty years in various rural areas of the kingdom and may indicate a tradition of rural production in earlier times.[18] *11in (28cm)*

14. Thirteenth-century bronze bracelet excavated in Benin from a mass burial ground along with numerous similar bronze objects. *5½in (14cm). Benin, National Museum*

collect oral traditions about this problem, but the results have been confusing because the investigators did not always ask the same questions nor did they interview the same people.[14] The version published by J. U. Egharevba, an Edo historian, is the best known and most utilized by scholars. It parallels the story of the origin of the royal dynasty by asserting that the arts of casting as well as those of ruling came from Ife:

> Oba Oguola [the fifth king] wished to introduce brass-casting into Benin so as to produce works of art similar to those sent him from Ife. He therefore sent to the Oni of Ife for a brass-smith and Iguegha(e) was sent to him.[15]

Unfortunately, it is not clear whether Egharevba's story is about the origin of the technique of casting, the introduction of specific objects, or the incorporation of one family into the casters' guild.

The guild of brass-smiths like many others in Benin, is composed of several lineages that have been incorporated at different times and have various origins, some even coming from outside the kingdom. The lineage of the senior title holder, the *Ineh*, maintains a tradition (which was probably the basis for Egharevba's published one) that until the time of Oba Oguola, brass-workers used to come from Ife every autumn to present their work to the king. Oba Oguola succeeded in enticing them to stay permanently in Benin and gave their leader, Iguegha, the title of *Ineh*.[17]

The family of the second-ranking title holder, the *Ihama*, claims, in contrast, to be autochthonous. According to the present Chief Ihama, brass-smiths already existed in *Ogiso* times but then produced only smaller objects such as bracelets and bells. In the fifteenth century, the Oba Ewuare introduced the casting of commemorative heads and other large objects and gave his family the title of *Ihama*. So traditions about brass-casting would seem to reflect the incorporation of families into guilds and the awarding of titles as much as they do the introduction of a technique or of a particular artistic form.

Archaeology so far has not yielded many answers about the origin of brass-casting in Benin. Only a few pre-European sites have been excavated and it is difficult to know whether they are representative. Nevertheless, the finds are important because they date to about the thirteenth and fourteenth centuries A.D. and consist of bronze objects – bracelets, rings and the like – which were made by smithing and chasing rather than being cast as were later Benin pieces. In other areas of West Africa hammering preceded casting as a technique for working copper metals and therefore these bronzes may be some of the earliest examples of Benin metalwork. There is a gap in the Benin archaeological record until the seventeenth and eighteenth centuries, and by then the lost-wax method of casting was generally in use.[19] Thus we do not know when casting was first employed in Benin. This technique was also used at the important artistic centres of Igbo Ukwu (ninth century) and Ife (fourteenth and fifteenth centuries) not far from Benin; however, the exact relationship between these three traditions is still to be determined.

Although these early pieces are made of bronze (an alloy mainly of copper and tin), most Benin sculpture so far tested has proven to be brass (copper and zinc).[20] Tin is found locally in Nigeria but copper is not, and so to make these early bronzes Benin must have been tied into a trading network in pre-European times. Archaeological finds of cowrie shells and glass beads dating from the same time are further evidence for trade links because this kind of cowrie shell comes from the east coast of Africa, while the beads could have come from Ife, a centre of glass-working by the early fourteenth century, or some yet undiscovered source. Thus, by about the thirteenth or fourteenth centuries Benin had entered commercial networks to acquire metal, shells, and beads for economic, cosmetic, artistic, or ritual uses.

15. A photograph taken by Northcote Thomas at the beginning of this century of an Igbo man. The hairstyle is similar to that of the brass trophy head in plate 16.[22]

The Age of the Warrior Kings: the 15th and 16th Centuries

The fifteenth and sixteenth centuries are crucial in Benin history. It is an age of conquest and artistic flowering. Many of the brass sculptural forms so characteristic of Benin art – commemorative, trophy, and Queen Mother heads as well as plaques and stools – are either mentioned for the first time in oral traditions about this period or are specifically attributed to obas who ruled then. This clustering of traditions makes it difficult not to see these two hundred years as critical to the development of art in Benin.

The fifteenth and sixteenth centuries was the period of the warrior kings: Ewuare, Ozolua, Esigie, Orhogbua, and Ehengbuda. It was a time of consolidation, development, and expansion of the kingdom. Benin oral history is full of tales of warfare and conquest, and the art is in part a reflection of the times (plates 16, 17 and 27). At its height, the kingdom extended in the west to Lagos, in the north-east to Ekiti and Owo, in the north-west throughout most of the Ishan area, and to the east up to the Niger River. However, 'the frontiers were continually expanding and contracting as new conquests were made and as vassals on the borders rebelled and were reconquered.'[21] During this period Benin notions of kingship – and the aesthetic ideas and objects associated with it – were spread over a large area as a result of practices such as sending royal brothers to rule over tributary areas, holding sons of conquered chiefs as hostages or trainees within the city, and sponsoring candidates for the thrones of groups under its sway. Specific objects, such as *ada* and brass masks (plate 17), were sent to vassal lords as emblems of their authority. Even in areas

16. Brass trophy head. The hairstyle of concentric rings, as well as the four supra-orbital tribal marks, are considered to be indications of a male foreigner. The casting of trophy heads may have originated a long time ago. In the Benin Museum there are two heads, one attributed to the reign of Oba Ozolua (late fifteenth or early sixteenth century) and one to the reign of Oba Akengbuda (late eighteenth century). According to Chief Ihama of the casters' guild: 'In the old days they used to cut off the head of [conquered] kings and bring it to the oba who would send it to our guild for casting. They did not necessarily cast heads of all the captured rulers, but just the most stubborn among them. If it happened that the senior son of a rebel king was put on the throne, the oba would send him the cast head of his father to warn him how his father was dealt with. In the old days these heads were kept on the Shrine of the Ancestors of the Benin Nation *(Edion Edo).'* *8¼in (21cm). Philadelphia, University of Pennsylvania Museum*

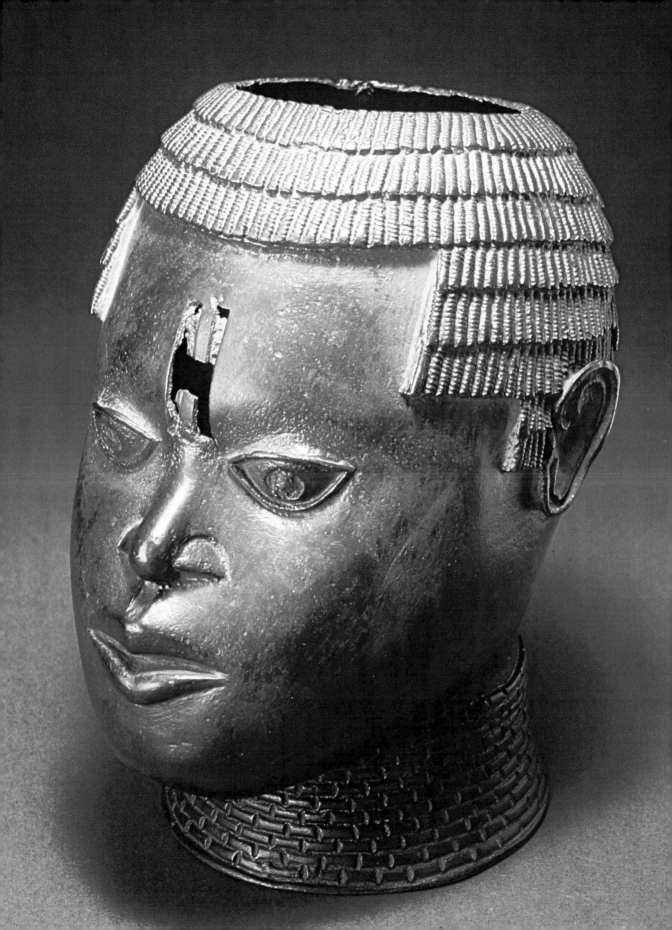

outside direct Benin control, like the Niger Delta, the reputation of the oba was such that leadership disputes were brought to him for arbitration and those who proved successful brought home Benin regalia.

The first of the warrior kings, the Oba Ewuare, who probably reigned in the mid-fifteenth century, looms large in Benin oral history. Even more than Oranmiyan and the early rulers of the dynasty, Ewuare set the patterns of Benin kingship. Under him Benin was transformed on every level, from its physical appearance to its religious and political organization. Ewuare's 'revolution' is expressed symbolically – whether or not it ever occurred in actuality – by his incineration of Benin City. Out of its ashes he constructed a new city and a new polity. Houses that were once built of poles or palm ribs padded with mud, like those of the south-eastern neighbours of Benin, were now constructed of courses of packed mud in a similar way to Yoruba houses. The palace, which had lacked a permanent site in previous reigns, was rebuilt on a large scale in the place where it has remained ever since. Under Ewuare the palace truly became the mystical and political hub of the nation.

Ewuare is credited with laying out the basic plan of the city (figure 2), with its roads radiating out of the centre as in Yoruba towns.[23] It is also supposed to have been Ewuare who divided the city into two parts – the oba's sector (*Ogbe*) and the town (*Ore ne Okhua*) – and organized the population of the capital into wards each characterized by the particular craft or ritual service which it owed the king. Ewuare is said to have constructed the inner wall or defensive earthwork of the city. Under each of its nine gates he placed magical charms to protect the kingdom from its enemies.

The restructuring of the city was paralleled by governmental reorganization. According to traditions, Ewuare established the three associations of Palace Chiefs, initiated lineal as opposed to collateral inheritance of the kingship, and made a number of other important innovations associated with a period of 'political centralization and administrative differentiation'.[24] At the same time, the Benin Empire began its period of expansion. Ewuare organized a 'war machine', which became an integral and permanent part of the state and thus extended the power of Benin far beyond its former borders.[25]

Similarly Ewuare is supposed to have established an annual cycle of royal ceremonies to protect and purify the nation. Most important of these were *Ugie Erha Oba*, in which the royal ancestors were honoured, and *Igue*, which was supposed to strengthen the mystical powers of the king. The elegant and elaborate ceremonial costumes worn by the king and chiefs also originated in Ewuare's time, in particular the coral bead regalia so important to kingship (plate 18).

17. Brass pendant worn by the Atah of Idah, king of the Igala. Traditions within the Igala royal family claim a Benin origin for the dynasty. The king (Atah) has several objects of clearly Benin origin to sanction his kingship: this 'bronze' mask (one of two), a 'bronze' cylindrical throne and an ornamental iron staff.[26] Masks of apparently Benin origin are found over a large area of Nigeria, indicating something of the Benin sphere of influence. *11½in (29cm). Possession of Atah of Idah*

18. Coral bead whisk. The beads of the oba are the emblem and essence of his office. He alone can wear a complete outfit of coral beads; chiefs (except the *Ezomo*) wear only necklaces, bracelets and anklets. In his wardrobe are many different styles of dress and headgear; indeed one of his praise names is 'Child of the beaded crown; child of the beaded gown'. *39½in (100cm). London, British Museum*

19. Brass figure of a Portuguese soldier. This figure in a distinctly provincial style was found, together with two similar ones, in Udo Village (compare with a soldier in the court style in plate 26). At the time of the British Expedition, there were eight brasses in the possession of the highest ranking chief of Udo, but three of them were taken by British officials. *13½in (34.5cm). Benin, National Museum*

20. (*Overleaf left*) Brass plaque, possibly sixteenth century. It represents an oba sacrificing a leopard, a ritual act performed at his coronation and at *Igue*, the annual ceremony dedicated to strengthening his mystical powers. Sacrifice of the leopard symbolizes the triumph of home over bush, for the oba as king of the settled land has proven himself superior to the leopard, king of the wilderness.
Representation of the oba as having mud-fish legs accomplishes his symbolic identification with Olokun, god of the great waters and source of all earthly wealth. The leopard is associated with the period before Ewuare assumed the throne. During his wanderings in exile, he slept one night under a tree and in the morning found a leopard above him on a branch. Ewuare took the leopard as a sign of future fortune and vowed that if ever he became king, he would sacrifice a leopard every year to his Head, the locus of his luck and power. The oba with mud-fish legs is often identified as Oba Ohen, the father of Ewuare, whose divine retribution for adultery was paralysis of the legs. When Ewuare wished to commemorate his father in brass, the casters depicted him in this way in order to disguise the deformity. *15½in (39.5cm). London, British Museum*

98
I–15
30.

XVII,1

21. *(Above)* **Brass plaque, probably sixteenth-century and representing Oba Esigie on his triumphant return from the Igala war. As he set out to battle, the prophetic bird cried out that disaster lay ahead. Esigie had the bird killed and proclaimed that 'whoever wishes to succeed in life should not heed the bird of prophecy'. Upon his return, he had the brass-casters make an image of the bird (plate 80).** *17in (43cm). London, British Museum*

In one story, Ewuare went down to the river at Ughoton Village and stole the beads belonging to Olokun, god of the waters; he brought them back to Benin and thereby established the palace of the oba, king of the dry land, as the earthly counterpart of the palace of Olokun, king of the waters. Thus, in Benin traditions, nearly every aspect of royal regalia and royal ritual is traced back to Ewuare, indicating that much of what is 'divine' in the divine kingship may have started at that time (plate 20).

The arts also flourished during his reign, particularly brass-casting. One popular story about Ewuare relates that when he had grown old he asked the members of both the casters' and carvers' guilds to make an image of him. The casters depicted him as he appeared at the prime of life, but the carvers showed him as he was at the time of the commission, in his old age. Ewuare was furious with the carvers and demoted them, proclaiming that they would never again be as important as the brass-workers. It is possible that this story is indirect evidence for the introduction of royal commemorative heads, as Chief Ihama of the brass-casters' guild feels it is. It certainly seems to reflect a change in guild hierarchy, for the carvers, organized during *Ogiso* times, should automatically rank higher than the casters, who were organized much later. The 'explanation' of their status reversal could well reflect changes in the cultural evaluation of artistic materials.

The sixteenth-century kings continued the patterns of conquest set by Ewuare, but their path was not always smooth. The reign of Esigie, the grandson of Ewuare and the fifteenth king, is marked in Benin traditions by two great conflicts, one internal and the other external. When Ozolua, the successor of Ewuare, died, a struggle for power ensued between his two sons, Esigie in Benin City and Aruaran in the town of Udo about twenty miles to the north-west. Udo at that time was an important centre, probably as large and powerful as Benin City, and its ruler apparently wished to make it the capital of the kingdom. According to Chief Ihama of the brass-casters' guild, during the conflict brass-casters were taken by force to Udo and worked there until Esigie won the war. In another account Udo is described as the temporary residence of brass-casters during their annual visit from Ife, before Oguola, the fifth oba, succeeded in enticing them to reside in Benin City. While these two traditions refer to different times and circumstances, both suggest a brief period of casting at Udo.[27]

Esigie's second major struggle was against the Igala people in the north, who are said to have attacked the kingdom, threatening its very existence. Benin oral literature abounds with stories about this war which Benin finally won, driving the Igala soldiers across the Niger River and apparently establishing their king, the *Ata*, as a vassal of Benin (plates 21 and 23). It is possible that the conflict with the Igala was over control of the Niger waterway.[28]

The fifteenth and sixteenth centuries are significant in Benin history, as well as that of West Africa generally, because they mark the first direct contact with the European world. In the second half of the fifteenth century, Portuguese navigators began to explore the West African coast and appear to have reached Benin sometime between 1472 and 1486. They found a highly developed kingdom in

22. The figures on this salt-cellar represent Portuguese horsemen, but they are portrayed in a distinctly Benin style. *11in (28cm). Copenhagen, National Museum of Denmark*

23. (*Above*) Queen Mother head. Idia, the mother of Oba Esigie, played an important role in his various successes, particularly the Igala war. In her honour Esigie is said to have instituted the title of Queen Mother, *Iye Oba*, and established the tradition of casting this type of brass head. The long beaded cap covers the distinguishing hair style of the Queen Mother, called 'chicken's beak'. According to Chief Ihama of the brass-casters' guild, the fish on the base may be a reference to Idia's efforts in chasing the Igala warriors across the Niger River. *20in (51cm). Berlin, Museum für Völkerkunde*

24. (*Above right*) Brass plaque of three traders, probably those appointed to deal with Europeans. The two on the sides hold manillas, an early form of trade currency. The figure in the centre is carrying a staff of office. The image of a crocodile grasping a fish is particularly appropriate, for the crocodile is considered the 'policeman' of the great waters, and represents power and control over the seas. It is probably sixteenth-century. *19¼in (49cm). London, British Museum*

the process of territorial conquest with whom they were able to establish diplomatic and trade relations. According to Benin traditions, the monarch ruling at that time was either Ozolua or, more likely, Esigie. The Portuguese hoped to introduce Christianity, particularly after they received reports that the Benin sovereignty was sanctioned by a ruler called the Ogane, living far into the interior, who sent the oba a bronze cross among other objects which confirmed his authority. Missionaries were dispatched but in the end Portuguese hopes for converts in Benin were not fulfilled.

The arrival of the Portuguese coincided with a period of great political and artistic development, as we have seen, and their coming probably acted as a catalyst in this process. Their impact was many-sided: military, economic, cultural, artistic, and even linguistic. Portuguese mercenaries provided Benin support against its enemies, while traders supplied the important luxury items Benin so desired: coral beads and cloth for ceremonial attire and great quantities of brass manillas which could be melted down for casting. One of the palace associations, *Iwebo*, was appointed to conduct affairs with the Portuguese and to this day its members speak a secret language that some of them claim is derived from Portuguese (plate 24).[29]

In return for these goods, Benin provided the Portuguese with pepper, cloth, ivory, and slaves. By the last quarter of the sixteenth

25. Benin court official holding a musket. This figure is probably a member of the *Iwoki* guild, a group concerned with unusual celestial phenomena like eclipses and comets. According to guild traditions, their founders were two Portuguese, Uti and Ava, who arrived during the reign of Oba Esigie. At the annual *Iron* ceremony the Iwoki stand on either side of the oba holding guns as his defenders. *Iron* commemorates the triumph of Oba Esigie over the rebellious Seven Uzama, a group of powerful chiefs.[30] *Probably eighteenth century. 17½in (44·5cm). Liverpool, Merseyside County Museums*

26. Portuguese soldier holding a matchlock. Portuguese soldiers and traders are depicted in Benin art wearing costumes and holding weapons dating mainly to the sixteenth century. European counterparts have been suggested for clothing worn by both Portuguese and Edo in the art.[31] *Probably sixteenth century. 15in (38cm). London, British Museum*

27. One of a series of plaques depicting Benin warriors in battle against their enemies, possibly the Igbo. *Probably sixteenth century. Leipzig, Museum für Völkerkunde*

century, if not earlier, Benin craftsmen were busy carving ivory objects ranging from spoons with handles carved in animal or bird form, sold at modest prices to sailors, to the more elaborate salt-cellars and hunting horns, destined apparently for the Portuguese nobility. The Edo were not alone in this enterprise, for other groups along the African coast in what is today Sierra Leone/Guinea Bissau, western Nigeria, and Zaire were similarly commissioned. The Benin-Portuguese ivories are a blending of status imagery from two cultures: from Europe, there are Portuguese coats of arms, armillary spheres, and scenes of the nobility hunting; from Benin, guild designs reserved for royalty, and views of nobles on horseback, accompanied by retainers and equipped with swords, elaborate costumes, feathers, and other Benin marks of rank and wealth.[32]

But the Portuguese also had an impact on the traditional art of Benin. Coming from far across the sea, bringing with them wealth and luxury items, the Portuguese travellers were readily incorporated into (or perhaps generated) the complex of ideas associated with the god Olokun, ruler of the seas and provider of earthly wealth. Cast or carved images of the Portuguese sailors in sixteenth-century attire appear in a wide variety of contexts – on bracelets, plaques, bells, pendants, masks, tusks, and so on. Generally they are accompanied by the denizens of Olokun's world (mudfish, crocodiles, pythons) and a multitude of chiefs, retainers, and royal figures of the Benin court. The image of the Portuguese, thus, became an integral part of a visual vocabulary of power and wealth (plates 25 and 26).

This can be seen most vividly in one art form: the brass plaque. In oral traditions, the earliest reference to the making of plaques is in the reign of Esigie and his son Orhogbua. A British official in 1897 was told that a caster named Ahammangiwa (a name of unclear origin) accompanied the Portuguese to Benin, making 'brasswork and plaques' first for Esigie and later for his son Orhogbua, to commemorate the successful war against the Igbo (plate 27). It is not clear whether this is a story about the origin of brasswork generally or of plaques specifically – or whether it is a story of origin at all. Whatever the case, it does indicate that plaque production was flourishing in the period of Portuguese contact. It is possible that the Portuguese introduced the notion of plaque making, perhaps, as one scholar suggests, by showing Benin casters small books of pictures. Indeed, some of the background designs on the plaques, such as the quatrefoil or rosette, may have European or even Islamic origins.[33]

There are over nine hundred plaques known and they provide a testimony to court life at that time. Although they are generally considered to be 'a sort of pictorial record of events in Benin history, an aid to memorizing oral traditions',[34] in fact very few of them convey narratives. Apart from the war plaques (plate 26) or the commemoration of Esigie's triumph over the Igala (plate 21), the majority represent kings, chiefs, and courtiers in ritual posture. Whatever narrative content they may have had has been lost. Their ritual content, however, can be partially reconstructed through the identification of costume (plates 76, 81, 85 and 97).

The plaques also appear to contain cosmological references intimately related to the Portuguese period. The background design on the majority of plaques is a quatrefoil, while on a minority there is a circled cross. Both of these patterns are associated now (and may well have been in the past) with Olokun, god of the waters. The quatrefoil

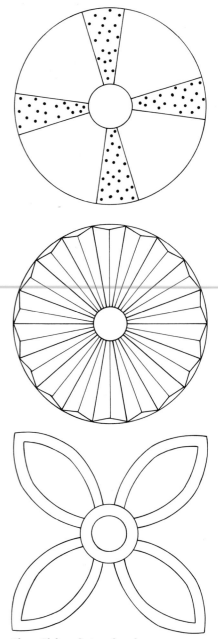

Three Olokun designs found on plaques. The one on top is called *aghadaghada* (a play on *ada* meaning 'crossroads'); in the middle *ebe-ame* ('river leaf'); bottom *owen iba ede ku* ('the sun never misses a day')

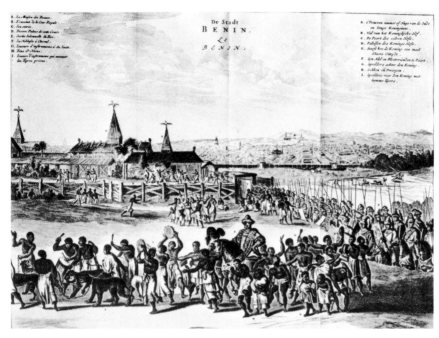

28. (*Above*) **A seventeenth-century Dutch engraving from Olfert Dapper's** *Nauwkeurige Beschrijvinge der Afrikaansche Gewesten,* **published in Amsterdam in 1668. Although this engraving apparently was made in Europe following verbal descriptions, there are nevertheless correspondences with what we know of Benin architecture. The turrets are described by other visitors and are depicted in Benin representations of the palace (plate 32). According to Dapper, 'The King shews himself only once a year to his people, going out of his court on horseback, beautifully attired with all sorts of royal ornaments, and accompanied by three or four hundred noblemen on horseback and on foot, and a great number of musicians before and behind him, playing merry tunes on all sorts of musical instruments, as is shown in the preceding picture of Benin City. Then he does not ride far from the court, but soon returns thither after a little tour. Then the king causes some tame leopards that he keeps for his pleasure to be led about in chains; he also shows many dwarfs and deaf people, whom he likes to keep at court.'**[36]

29. (*Above right*) **A brass figure of a dwarf, a member of the oba's entourage as described by Dapper (plate 28).** *Vienna, Museum für Völkerkunde*

represents river leaves,[35] which are used by Olokun priestesses in curing rites, and the circled cross is one form of the *aghadaghada* design drawn in chalk at the centre of all Olokun shrine courtyards. Both the leaf and the circled cross are quadrivial, a basic cosmological form in Benin thought. Called *Ede enene*, the cruciform represents simultaneously the four cardinal directions, the four days of the week, and the unfolding of the day – morning, afternoon, evening, and night – at the time of creation. In the corners of many plaques are designs similarly relating to Olokun: Portuguese heads, crocodiles, fish, and rosettes, which represent the sun, associated with Olokun through its daily descent into the sea. The appearance of so much Olokun imagery as background in plaques depicting court ritual and court life is a perfect commentary on the period of Esigie's reign, when the powers of the sea worked behind the oba to strengthen and expand the kingdom.

Crisis and Renewal: the Seventeenth and Eighteenth Centuries

While the Portuguese impact was strong it was nonetheless brief, for they were soon surpassed in trade by the Dutch, French, and English. Visitors throughout the seventeenth and early eighteenth centuries have provided us with a vivid picture of the size and complexity of Benin City and of the customs, ceremonies, costumes, and art forms associated with Benin life both at court and at large. Indeed, we find in a Spanish Capuchin letter of 1651–52 the very first description, however unfavourable, of a domestic ancestral altar:

> Every man whether great or small, and according to his means, has within his house an altar or shrine well adorned with hideous idols, bones, skulls of cows, pigs, monkeys, crocodiles, rotten eggs, and other vile things; they also have some heads, like those of goats, each of which holds a very large elephant tusk. And there are some

30 and 31. Brass stool, identified as the one commissioned by Oba Eresonyen. On the base are images drawn from the bush and water (monkeys and frogs) as well as the sign of the powerful hand. At the centre is a circle which is probably a blacksmith's anvil, surrounded on either side by blacksmith's tools and ceremonial swords. Above these symbols of civilization are cosmic symbols (a moon, Maltese cross, and sun) and below are symbols of the bush (a monkey's head and two elephant trunks ending in hands holding magical leaves). *15½in (39·5cm). Berlin, Museum für Völkerkunde*

holes, in front of which are carved the devil and various other things, according to the devotion of each person.[37]

The various objects described, including the 'goat head', actually a wooden ram (plate 41), can all be found on paternal ancestral altars today.

Dutch descriptions of the royal palace and its art works are of particular interest because this important edifice was destroyed by fire in 1897 and thus we can only know about it indirectly through these accounts and artistic depictions. In the writings of Olfert Dapper, who used early seventeenth-century Dutch reports as his sources, we find the earliest European depiction (plate 28) and written description of the palace:

> The king's court is square, and stands at the right hand side when entering the town by the gate of Gotton [Ughoton], and is certainly as large as the town of Haarlem, and entirely surrounded by a special wall, like that which encircles the town. It is divided into many magnificent palaces, houses, and apartments of the courtiers, and comprises beautiful and long square galleries, about as large as the Exchange at Amsterdam, but one larger than another, resting on wooden pillars, from top to bottom covered with cast copper, on which are engraved the pictures of their war exploits and battles, and are kept very clean. Most palaces and the houses of the king are covered with palm leaves instead of square pieces of wood, and every roof is decorated with a small turret ending in a point, on which birds are standing, birds cast in copper with outspread wings, cleverly made after living models.[38]

Some sixty years later, a Dutch visitor, David Van Nyandael, saw the same complex of apartments and galleries. His is the first description of a royal ancestral altar, of much the same form as we know today, and while he does not mention either the 'copper' birds or plaques, he does point out for the first time the cast snakes that ran along the turrets:

> on top of the last [gate] is a wooden turret, like a chimney, about sixty or seventy foot high. A large copper snake is attached to its top, its head dangling downwards. This snake is so neatly cast with all its curves and everything that I can say that this is the finest thing I have seen in Benin . . . [In another gallery] one sees behind a white carpet eleven human heads cast in copper; upon each of these is an elephant's tooth, these being some of the King's gods.[39]

We cannot know if the differences between the accounts by Dapper and Van Nyandael are due to omissions in reporting or changes in artistic use in the last years of the seventeenth century. It has been suggested, however, that the absence of reference to the brass plaques in the latter's account indicates that they were no longer being made by 1702.[40]

In looking at the history of Benin in the seventeenth century we find a curious contrast between an abundance of Dutch and other written descriptions and a complete paucity of local oral traditions. While the exploits of the fifteenth and sixteenth-century warrior kings are related in great detail, little is recounted of their successors, approximately nine kings, starting with the son of the last great warrior oba, Ehengbuda (who probably reigned in the late sixteenth century) and ending with the ascension of Akenzua I in about 1715. Similarly, there are no art historical traditions related to this period; no objects are said to have been introduced by specific obas and there

32 *(Above)* **A brass plaque showing a palace entrance with a turret. Here the bird, snake, and possibly plaques appear together, in contrast to the differing seventeenth-century Dutch accounts. The body of the bird, which is broken off, has outstretched wings and a curved beak similar to the staff illustrated in plates 21 and 80. It may represent the prophetic bird, or another of similar powers, for its role on the palace roof is to ward off danger. The snake descending the turret is a python. Such snakes were seen by visitors from the eighteenth century on and a number of heads** *(above right)* **and some segments remain. The python is the king of the snakes and a messenger of the god Olokun, ruler of the great waters. Here it protects the palace of Olokun's counterpart, the king of the dry land. The pillars supporting the turret have representations of Portuguese heads, which may be the plaques seen by Dapper or the carved wooden pillars seen by van Nyandael and others.** *Plaque: 20½in (52cm). Berlin, Museum für Völkerkunde. Python head: 16¼in (41·4cm). Philadelphia, University of Pennsylvania Museum*

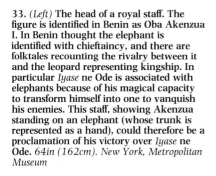

33. *(Left)* **The head of a royal staff. The figure is identified in Benin as Oba Akenzua I. In Benin thought the elephant is identified with chieftaincy, and there are folktales recounting the rivalry between it and the leopard representing kingship. In particular** *Iyase* **ne Ode is associated with elephants because of his magical capacity to transform himself into one to vanquish his enemies. This staff, showing Akenzua standing on an elephant (whose trunk is represented as a hand), could therefore be a proclamation of his victory over** *Iyase* **ne Ode.** *64in (162cm). New York, Metropolitan Museum*

are no tales containing reference to the use of artistic forms. At the most, a few seventeenth-century kings can be tentatively identified in the plaques (plate 35). The situation changes dramatically when we come to the eighteenth-century obas, Akenzua I and his son Eresonyen. Here the numerous traditions emphasize the great peace and artistic flowering of the first half of the eighteenth century. It is possible to comprehend this curious silence and the sudden flourishing of the arts that followed – and even the specific art forms that emerged – when we understand something of the background of seventeenth-century Benin.

The seventeenth century was a period of great internal turmoil. After the death of Ehengbuda, the last warrior king, his son Ohuan ascended the throne. 'Ohuan did not reign for a long time before he died and because he had no children he did not hand down royal tradition to his successor.'[41] Thus, with his death, the Oranmiyan dynasty ended and in its place came a series of kings whose ancestry and claim to the throne of Benin are in shadow. Without the legitimacy of Oranmiyan origins, the kingship itself was seriously weakened and powerful rebel chiefs struggled to have control over it. The task facing Akenzua I and Eresonyen thus was two-fold: to subdue rebellious chiefs and to restore the power and legitimacy of the monarchy. The art forms associated with these obas are a testimony to their efforts and ultimate success.

Oral traditions indicate that both Akenzua I and Eresonyen sought to strengthen the kingship through a combination of political, economic, and ritual means. During the preceding century, independent chiefs had succeeded in establishing private power bases and apparently had even selected kings from among their ranks.[42] At the turn of the century, a particularly strong *Iyase* (head of the Town Chiefs and one of two supreme military commanders) was involved in a rebellion against Oba Ewuakpe and, after his death, supported a rival brother of Akenzua I. This rebel chief, the *Iyase* ne Ode, appears in Benin oral literature as a threatening foe and a magician so powerful that he was able to transform himself into an elephant. His legendary association with elephants is particularly apt since the *Iyase* ne Ode's power base was centred at the village of Oregbeni, the home of the elephant hunters' guild.[43] In fact, it is quite possible that the struggle between *Iyase* ne Ode and the oba was over control of the lucrative ivory trade that began at the end of the seventeenth century. With the aid of the other major military commander, the *Ezomo*, Oba Akenzua I at last defeated the *Iyase* and then went on to establish firmly the rule of primogeniture, thus ensuring stability in royal succession. Celebration of this victory over the *Iyase* and of the restoration of the monarchy is the theme of the elaborate brass staff of office attributed by tradition to Akenzua I.

Increased trade with the Dutch – whether it was a result or a cause of Akenzua's strengthened position – ushered in an era of great prosperity. Ivory was a particularly important export, as Dutch trade records indicate. On the Benin side, there was a similar emphasis on luxury goods. Cowries, the traditional currency, were imported in such great quantities that they literally covered the walls of the rich. Oba Akenzua I is said to have constructed a 'house of money' and this apparently was emulated, perhaps in a modified form, by the *Ezomo*, for when the French trader Landolphe visited Benin in 1787, he met the then *Ezomo* in 'a large and beautiful room elegantly embedded with small Indian shells ... which are called cauris'.[44] Traces of this decorative practice can still be seen in Benin today (plate 4).

In addition to cowries, a variety of cloth including damask, French silk, and linen, and a vast number of copper and brass 'neptunes' or pans were also imported.[45] A portion of the latter was undoubtedly melted down to cast the numerous brass objects said to date from that time. It should be no surprise that one of the art forms *par excellence* of the century was the brass *ikegobo*, shrine of the Hand. The shrine of the Hand is the ultimate self-congratulation of the individual who has achieved great material success. Two elaborate brass *ikegobo* are attributed to this time, one of which, now in the British Museum, was undoubtedly made for the oba, while the other belonged, appropriately, to *Ezomo*, his loyal and powerful chief (plate 34).

Restoration of the kingship nevertheless brought fundamental changes in its character. 'The revival could not carry the monarch and government back to the forms of the sixteenth century. Akenzua and his successors confined themselves within the palace ... and maintained their authority ... by an increasing emphasis upon their ritual function as guardians of the nation's prosperity and security'[46] (plate 36).

Perhaps even more than Akenzua, Eresonyen developed the ceremonial aspects of kingship. To this end he forged artistic and ritual

34. (*Above*) **Brass shrine of the Hand belonging to Chief** *Ezomo*. **Within the** *Ezomo* **family, this** *ikegobo* **is said to have been cast for Ehenua, the** *Ezomo* **who aided Oba Akenzua I in conquering** *Iyase* **ne Ode: however, scholars feel that on stylistic grounds the main body of the casting, but probably not the base, may be from a later date.**
The iconography of the *ikegobo* **refers to the conflict. On the top is Akenzua I 'making offerings to his ancestors for the success of his campaign, or giving thanks for victory'. The animals he has sacrificed form the frieze around the base. The central figure on the cylinder is** *Ezomo* **Ehenua, the founder of the present** *Ezomo* **line, surrounded by his warriors and attendants.**[47] *16in (40·5cm)*

35. (*Right*) **Brass plaque of a procession. This plaque is associated in Benin today with Oba Ewuakpe, the last of the weak seventeenth-century kings, because of the appearance of an** *akpata* **(bow-lute) player in the upper right-hand corner. Ewuakpe was said to have played this instrument to console himself during the long period when his subjects were in revolt. However, this identification may well be anachronistic if the production of plaques did end in the mid-seventeenth century.** *17in (43cm). Cleveland, Museum of Art*

37. *(Right)* This type of equestrian figure may be the 'blacksmith on an ass' referred to in the anonymous account in the *Royal Gold Coast Gazette*. This particular sculpture is one of the few pieces of Benin brass art to be taken out before the Expedition. It belonged to a British merchant, J. H. Swainson and was given to him as a wedding gift by Oba Ovoranmwen in about 1892.[48] The equestrian figure may represent Oranmiyan, the founder of the second dynasty, who introduced horses into Benin. The fact that such figures were placed on ancestral altars (plate 38) seems to support this identification. However, it has been suggested that it represents Oronmila, the Yoruba god of divination, or alternatively, because of the headdress, an emissary from the north.[49] The figure has been dated by thermoluminescence to 1560 ± 40. *18¼in (46·5cm). Liverpool, Merseyside County Museums*

36. *(Left)* Osun cult head. The symbolism of the figures on this cast head refer to the mystical and magical aspects of kingship so emphasized by the eighteenth-century obas. The birds, celts, and snakes are all attributes of the cult of Osun, the power inherent in leaves and herbs found in the bush. Celts, or thunder-stones, are associated not only with Osun but also with Ogiuwu, bringer of death, who hurtles them down from the sky on his enemies. The birds are similar to those depicted on the top of the palace and have the same prophetic and protective powers. Snakes are the warriors of Osun. The representations of snakes issuing from nostrils refers to the belief that those who are magically powerful vomit out snakes when setting out to destroy their enemies. On stylistic grounds this head is dated to the early eighteenth century, which corresponds with the recent thermoluminiscent date of 1710 ± 35.[50] *10¾in (27cm). London, British Museum*

links with earlier periods of the monarchy and with its most basic sanctions. Eresonyen is said to have commissioned a brass stool (plate 30) in the exact form of one made for Esigie by the Portuguese two hundred years earlier. There are indeed parallels between Esigie and Eresonyen: both overcame serious internal opposition and, thanks to a thriving trade with Europeans, ruled over a wealthy and powerful kingdom. In each reign brass-casting flourished. The emulation of Esigie was clearly an appeal to a time when the kingdom was at its height, led by a successful monarch of undeniably legitimate ancestry.

Just as Esigie had introduced a new palace ritual, *Ugie Oro*, into the annual cycle, so Eresonyen introduced *Ugie Ododua*, but his purpose

Sketch of
The Burying Place of a King of Benin

This is done by Belzonie the Traveller

was not strictly commemorative. *Ododua* was brought in as a replacement for the annual ceremony of the *Ovia* cult, honouring a village-based deity. At the *Ovia* rite (as performed in villages today), masqueraders wearing red parrot-feather head-dresses impersonate their patrilineal ancestors. In contrast, at *Ododua* (named after the Ife king who sent his son Oranmiyan to Benin as ruler) the performers, wearing brass helmet masks, represent the palace gods Uwen and Ora and their followers who came from Ife with Oranmiyan (plates 98, 100, 101). In replacing *Ovia* with *Ododua*, Eresonyen was not only emphasizing the royal lineage as opposed to more general ancestors but was appealing to the Yoruba progenitor of the Benin royal house, that is, to the ultimate legitimacy of the Oranmiyan dynasty.

Before the Fall: The Eighteenth and Nineteenth Centuries

The late eighteenth and early nineteenth-century successors of Eresonyen inherited a stable, prosperous, and moderately expansionist

38. *(Above) Sketch of the burying place of the king of Benin.* The explorer Belzoni, who visited Benin in 1823, appears to have written the legend to this sketch, but there is doubt as to whether he actually did the drawing. The depiction on 'one of 25 or 30 of the Tombs of the Benin Kings' accords with the anonymous description in the *Royal Gold Coast Gazette.* From the sketch it is possible to identify many types of object, many of which had not been recorded as being placed on ancestral altars (plates 37, 39 and 40). *Collection J. Hewett*

39. *(Right)* **Brass commemorative head.** The elaborate collars on these commemorative heads represent the coral bead headgear and chokers worn by Benin kings at the main annual rituals. The winged projections on the cap represent the ceremonial sword, *ada. Philadelphia, University of Pennsylvania Museum*

kingdom. After the ivory trade with the Dutch ceased, increased commerce in slaves and palm oil with the British developed in its place. One result of this relationship with England was that Benin became an object of the Victorian interest in exploration. Two great explorers, Sir Richard Burton and Giovanni Belzoni, visited Benin, and from them and others we have invaluable documents on its culture and art. Their accounts provide us with the last – and sometimes the only – picture of Benin royal sculpture before it was totally removed from its cultural context at the time of the 1897 British Punitive Expedition. In addition, when compared with earlier Dutch and French reports, their descriptions provide an important historical perspective on artistic developments over several hundred years.

The royal ancestral altars have long been a focus of artistic elaboration, perhaps even dating back to *Ogiso* times. Much of the sculptural forms that most characterize Benin art were originally created to honour the royal ancestors of the Benin nation. After the death of an oba, his successor would have an altar constructed in a large rectangular compound and would commission his carvers and casters to prepare art works to commemorate his predecessor and to enable the new oba to communicate with him. Thus, the number of shrine compounds was normally on the increase and by the first quarter of the nineteenth century, twenty-five or thirty of them were reported by a European visitor (plate 38). The number may have fluctuated with the degree of interest expressed by the reigning monarch, because at the time of the British Punitive Expedition in 1897, there were only seventeen.[51] Similarly, the types of artistic decoration may have varied from shrine to shrine and over time.

In the early eighteenth century, Van Nyandael saw on one altar 'eleven men's heads cast in copper . . . and upon every one of these is an elephant's tooth'. On another he saw only carved tusks, a variant of altar decoration seen also by French and English visitors from the late eighteenth through to the late nineteenth century.[52] Yet from the early 1820s we have both a written description (by an anonymous author in the *Royal Gold Coast Gazette*) and, perhaps even more remarkable, an actual sketch of a Benin altar (plate 38) with many other brass objects represented. According to the account:

> The tombs are decorated by as many large elephant's teeth as can be set in the space; these are elegantly carved in the manner of the ancients, and the socket of the tooth is introduced into the crown of the head of a colossal brazen bust, that by its correctness of expression and regularity of features confirms our opinion of that art having been long introduced and liberally cultivated by those people. The drapery, which resembles the collar of a large toga or

40. *(Above)* This type of figure may be the 'carpenter in the act of striking with an axe' recorded in the anonymous *Royal Gold Coast Gazette* account. The 'axe' in question is the blacksmith's hammer, *avalaka.* Scholars often identify the figure as a messenger from Ife, although in Benin it is considered to be a representation of the priest of Osanobua, the creator god. The cross worn around the figure's neck is a cosmological symbol referring to the creation of the world. *25in (63·5cm).* *Philadelphia, University of Pennsylvania Museum*

41. Carved ram's head. In Benin City today, no one recalls the use of these figures on ancestral altars, but some are still found in villages throughout the kingdom. *14in (35·5cm). London, British Museum*

91259

large gown covers part of the cheek, according to the ancient
costume of Egypt, and in fact the whole is in the best style of
workmanship. The other figures on these monuments are very
happy, a blacksmith on an ass, and a carpenter in the act of striking
with an axe, are well portrayed, and figures of animals are
generally equally happy in design and execution.[53]

Later, a member of the Punitive Expedition was to record some of the
same brass figures on the altars.[54] Whether the accumulation of
free-standing statuary is a nineteenth-century development or our
knowledge of it is merely a result of selective viewing by earlier visitors
is difficult to determine.

In 1862, when Sir Richard Burton visited Benin City, he spent
some time in a chief's house and has left a very detailed description of
what was principally a paternal ancestral altar:

The domestic altar is 'rigged up' in various ways, too various in fact
for short description. Some are external, provided with all the
heterogeneous mixture of idols: waterpots, pipkins of spirits,
cowries, chalk-sticks, ivories, some elaborately and beautifully
carved as the Chinese, men's heads coarsely imitated in wood and
metal, cocoa-nuts, and huge red clay pipes of Benin make.[55]

This is not the earliest description of a chief's altar, for the Capuchins (in 1651–52) and Landolphe and his party (in 1787) preceded him. There is, however, a significant difference in their accounts: while the earlier Spanish and French visitors saw what they described as heads of 'goats', 'billy goats' or 'rams' (plate 42), Burton saw a carved human representation. This difference is, in fact, a confirmation of the Benin oral tradition that during the reign of Oba (c.1816) chiefs petitioned the king to change their altar decoration to human commemorative heads in wood, an 'inferior' material but an equivalent form to the brass heads used by the king,[56] Burton's 1862 account, then, appears to document this change.

By the time Burton was there, and for the following thirty years, Benin's fortunes were in decline. Its political and economic hold on its tributaries was seriously weakened by conflicts along its northern and eastern borders and incursions by the British from the coast. In short, 'the reign of Adolo saw Benin driven back into the original Edo heartland'.[57] The British viewed Benin as the main obstacle in their expansion into the agricultural interior and when, in 1897, an envoy to the oba was ambushed and killed, the British sent out a punitive expedition against the kingdom. Their capture of the city and subsequent exile of the oba marked the end of Benin as an independent kingdom and the beginning of a new era of social, political, and artistic change (plate 42).

During the siege, many inhabitants of Benin City – the craftsmen included – fled to the villages and farms. With the oba gone, the traditional impetus for artistic creation no longer existed and art production stagnated. The situation changed dramatically, however, when in 1914 the British allowed Oba Eweka II, the senior son of the last independent king, to assume the throne. Upon his ascension, Eweka faced the challenge of restoring the kingship. One of his first projects was the reconstruction of the palace to some of its former glory, a task for which he needed the traditional craftsmen. Carvers and casters were put to work producing replacements for the shrine objects taken during the Expedition (plate 68).[58]

In 1914 he also lifted the restrictions on the sale of art work and built a shed, later to become an Arts and Crafts School, in the palace courtyard so that the craftsmen could have a place to work and sell their wares. Traditional guild members were thus able to continue creating art forms for their former patrons while at the same time producing objects for a new clientele: colonial officers, tourists, and a developing Western-educated Nigerian elite. At the same time the government schools introduced art classes based on Western techniques and styles. In this way, new approaches to art and new forms have emerged in Benin in the twentieth century as a complex reaction to a changing situation.[59]

Art, Belief and Ritual

43. *(Left)* Mud shrine in Benin City dedicated to Olokun in the home of the priestess Igheghian Uwangue and made by her husband Iyamu Ehigiato. Osanobua appears to the right of the central figure, Olokun. The mud construction is covered with lead paint as a symbol of permanence, as expressed in the Edo saying: 'Lead never rots, brass never rusts'

44. *(Below)* Olokun ritual pot. Not all Olokun pots are decorated with figures, but all share the same basic shape: squat and full-formed body, narrow top, and incised ornamental lugs. The figures on decorated pots represent scenes of Olokun worship: priestesses, musicians, devotees who have received the major gift of Olokun, children. The pythons which descend across the rim are the messengers of the god. *Private collection*

In Benin cosmology there is a basic dichotomy between two planes of existence: the visible, tangible world of everyday life (*agbon*) and the invisible spirit world (*erinmwi*), inhabited by the creator god, other deities, spirits, and supernatural powers. These are two parallel co-existing realms. Their boundaries, however, are not inviolable, as gods and spirits daily intervene in the lives of humans, and particularly powerful men draw upon the forces of the spirit world to transform daily experience. The relationship between these two spheres constitutes the dynamic of Benin religion.

The world as it is known to the Edo – the cosmological realms, geographical borders, and sociopolitical hierarchies – was created by Osanobua, the high god. In the beginning there was no land, only primordial waters. At the centre of the waters stood a tree and on its top lived *Owonwon*, the toucan. When Osanobua decided to populate the world, he gathered his three sons and sent them off in a canoe. Each was given the choice of one gift to take with him. The two elder sons chose wealth and craft tools. As the youngest prepared to choose his own gift, *Owonwon* cried out to him to take a snail shell. This he did, and when the canoe reached the centre of the waters, the youngest son turned the shell upside down and out poured an endless stream of sand. In this manner, the land began to emerge from the waters. The sons of Osanobua were afraid to go out from the canoe, and so the chameleon was sent to test the firmness of the ground. From that time on, it walks with a hesitating step. The place where the land emerged was called Agbon, 'the world', a name since changed to Agbor, today an Igbo town to the east of Benin City. At Agbon, Osanobua first came down from the sky on a chain and demarcated the world. It was from there he sent people to the four corners of the earth, to every country and geographic realm. He made his youngest son the ruler of Benin, the owner of the land. And he established his own realm, the spirit world, across the waters where the sky and earth meet.

Osanobua is envisaged as living in a magnificent palace, surrounded by courtiers and served by other deities. But for mankind he is a remote god, primarily concerned with the spirit world, having delegated his children to care for the world of everyday life. There are no organized groups worshipping him, no regular meetings and no public priesthood. Prayers to him open every religious service, but these are primarily formulaic, gestures of worship rather than active requests. Osanobua is appealed to only as a last resort, when all else fails. Unlike the other gods and spirits he never demands human sacrifice, a sign that he is remote as well as utterly benevolent.

In the front courtyard of most compounds is a shrine to Osanobua called *Osagbaye*. It is not elaborate, consisting only of a long pole stuck into a mound of sand. At the top of the pole is a pure white cloth which flutters in the breeze like a flag. The shrine evokes the creation myth: a solitary tree in the sand emerging from the primordial waters. The white sand and cloth are cool, peaceful, ritually pure.

While Osanobua is like other African creator gods in that he is removed from daily life, he differs from them most radically in that he is actually depicted in the art. Images of Osanobua appear in the form of *Ekpo* cult masks[60] and as life-size mud figures in shrines dedicated to his senior son, Olokun, lord of the great waters (plate 43). It is interesting to note that in these shrines, Osanobua is seated to the rear of Olokun in a clearly subordinate position. In the Benin adage, 'One can indeed bear a child greater than oneself as Osanobua bore Olokun.'

Olokun is the most popular and widely worshipped deity in Benin. His role is indeed greater than that of his father. In Benin cosmology, Olokun is identified with the great oceans of the earth which surround the land and into which all the rivers flow. More specifically, he is associated with the Ethiope (Olokun) River in the south-eastern part of the kingdom, which is considered the source of all the global waters. The path to the spirit world lies across the sea and the souls of those who have died, as well as those about to be born, must pass over the water. It is this last association which explains why Olokun is considered to be the provider of children to the Edo, for whom large families are a source of wealth and prestige. Olokun is similarly considered the source of riches and good fortune since before making this crossing the soul is blessed by him, ensuring luck, wealth, and success. It has been suggested that the particular association of Olokun with wealth may be due to the coming of European trading ships across the sea.[61] In offering children, health, and wealth to his followers, Olokun differs perhaps in degree but not in kind from other Benin deities. But in one area he differs completely and that is his demand for beauty in all its forms: graceful movement in dance, 'sweet' songs, elaborate shrine decoration, rich fabrics, and, most of all, beautiful women. Especially beautiful women are said to have been sent to earth by Olokun as his special devotees.

Although both men and women are worshippers of Olokun, he is widely considered in Benin to be the special concern of women because of his role in providing children. Parents of a female child install a small shrine to Olokun for her protection and future well-being. At the time of marriage, a woman transfers this shrine to her husband's house, where it assumes even greater importance with her new married status. The shrine consists of a whitewashed mud altar upon which are placed pieces of kaolin chalk, a symbol of purity and good luck, and a special ritual pot containing fresh river water (plate 44). These pots are made by women in various villages specializing in

45. (*Above*) **Sketch of brass kola nut box. Kola nuts are a major feature of offerings, both in rituals and for hospitality. Chiefs and commoners have wooden kola-nut boxes but a brass one such as this probably belonged to the king. The fluted gourd is the characteristic oblation to Osanobua, to whom it is offered in lieu of a cow, the highest level of domestic animal sacrifice. This container, thus, is a visual play on the concept of offering.** *Formerly Pitt Rivers collection*

46 and 47. **Olokun rattle staff, with detail showing the figure on the top** (*far right*)**. Special rattle staffs** (*ukhurhe*) **carved by the urban guild are used in village Olokun rituals. The** *ukhurhe* **of this cult are characterized by the figure of a priest on top and of a woman kneeling, holding an offering of kola nuts, in the middle segment.** *58⅞in (149·5cm). Copenhagen, National Museum of Denmark*

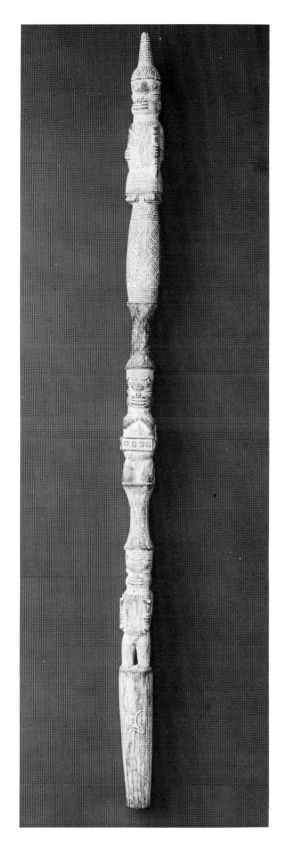

pottery making, by female members of the urban brass casters' guild, or by cult priestesses who have been 'chosen' by the deity for this craft activity. While all traditional women in Benin have Olokun altars in their homes, some of them become particularly involved in his worship because of health or sexual problems, difficulties in conception, or a 'calling' expressed in states of possession. These women join local cult groups which are headed by a master priestess and which meet every week for purification and possession rituals. A man with similar problems might also seek help through cult membership but will rarely become as actively involved.

In the area of Iyekorhionmwon near the Ethiope (Olokun) River, the worship of Olokun is organized on a village level. All members of the village, male and female, participate, with the oldest man often designated as chief priest. In many of these villages there are elaborate mud shrines of up to forty life-sized figures (plate 48). These tableaux depict the palace of Olokun under the sea, a kind of paradise of purity, beauty, joy and wealth. All the beautiful women and children are there, to be sent by the god to his devotees on earth. Also there is the storehouse for all the riches of the world, including most notably the coral beads which adorn the king of Benin, and give him his authority.

At the centre of these altars stands the figure of Olokun, larger than life, his arms supported in the traditional ceremonial stance of deference. As the senior son of Osanobua, and ruler in his own right of a vast realm, Olokun is represented in the form of a Benin king in full

48. *(Left)* **Olokun shrine in Evboesi Village**

49. *(Left)* **Wooden statue of Esu in Benin City.** *(Above)* **Brass plaque of the messenger of the god of death. Representations of Ofoe are most commonly and appropriately found on ancestral altars. On plaques such as this, which would have been part of the decoration of the palace, the figure symbolized the king's power of life and death over his subjects.** *18½in (47cm).*
Lagos, National Museum

ceremonial regalia. Particular emphasis is placed on his beads, which are famous in oral tradition for their beauty and abundance. Behind the king stand his wives and female attendants and to his side his numerous chiefs and courtiers. The range of different personages portrayed varies from shrine to shrine, but can include court musicians, jesters, peace officers, executioners, lame gatekeepers, soldiers, and various titled chiefs. Mud shrines of this type, but with fewer figures, are found also in the homes of chiefs in Benin City, where they are but one part of a series of altars dedicated to various deities and mystical powers, and represent their owners' wealth and rank. Within recent times, chief priestesses of urban cult groups have also begun to erect mud altars in response, they say, to demands by the god.

Olokun and his father, Osanobua, are considered 'cool' gods, that is, they represent the positive aspects of experience: ritual purity, good luck, health, long life, prosperity, and happiness, all symbolized by the colour white. In sharp contrast stand Ogiuwu, bringer of death, and Esu, gatekeeper of the gods, who stimulates confusion and wrongdoing in the affairs of men. Symbolized by the colour black, these deities are associated with nighttime, mourning, evil omens, and the ritual pollution which causes disease. Ogiuwu is no longer worshipped in Benin and it is difficult today to learn much about his cult in former times. A shrine once existed in the central part of town where many human sacrifices were offered. Ogiuwu is said to be the owner of the blood of all living things. He uses sacrificial blood to wash down the walls of his palace, and has a particular preference for that of humans. While Ogiuwu himself never appears in artistic form, his messenger Ofoe does (left). Ofoe is sent by Ogiuwu to take human life and thus he is represented as the pursuer, a figure with no body, only legs with which to chase his victim and arms with which to capture him. 'Ofoe has no mercy and yields to no sacrifice or entreaty.'[62]

As the worship of Ogiuwu fades, that of Esu becomes stronger, perhaps because transition and confusion far better characterize modern times than human sacrifice. Esu is said to have been so harsh in character and so untrustworthy that he was removed from the family of Osanobua and placed outside by the gate, where he waits, holding the key to the spirit world. A small wooden image of Esu (plate 49) is placed in the front of some compounds, its back towards the residence, its face turned out to the street. There, too, Esu is a gatekeeper, whose role is to cause havoc among those who may threaten the occupants of the house he protects.

Just as the colour white symbolizes the qualities of Osanobua and Olokun and black those of Esu and Ogiuwu, so red embodies and expresses the nature of Ogun and Osun. These deities are associated with sudden and violent action, anger, fire, and blood. As the middle

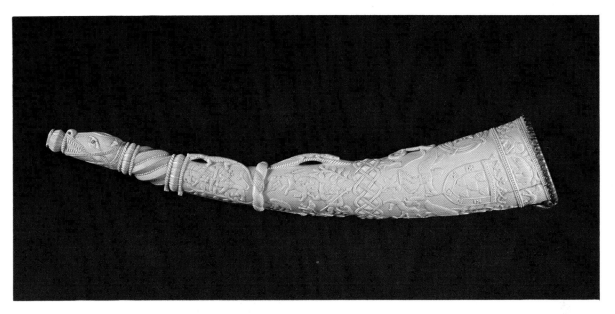

50. *(Left)* **A figure of Ogun in an Olokun mud shrine in Benin City. Ogun's tools decorate his red skirt and around his neck hang the iron bells used by his priests in rituals**

51. *(Top)* **Osun ivory horn. Osun specialists use these horns, made of ivory or wood, to announce to the witches that a ceremony is about to begin.** *London, British Museum*

52. *(Above)* **Brass cup used by Osun specialists for** *Ewawa* **divination. Small brass images of humans, animals, cowries and other objects are shaken in the cup and thrown down into a drum. The resulting arrangements of images are then analyzed.** *Vienna, Museum für Völkerkunde*

term in the symbolic triad, Ogun and Osun partake of both the beneficent qualities of Osanobua and Olokun and the harmful potentials of Esu and Ogiuwu. Theirs is an ambivalent nature in the literal meaning of the term for they are equally as capable of inflicting instant death as providing health and riches.

Ogun is the patron of farmers, craftsmen, hunters, and warriors – all who depend on tools. In Benin thought, Ogun is conceived in both abstract and anthropomorphic forms. As an abstract concept, Ogun represents the force inherent in metal, a mystical power with the potential to create or destroy. In this capacity, Ogun cannot be artistically represented except indirectly through those objects in which the power of metal resides, such as ceremonial swords (plate 11) or proclamation staffs (plate 70). Ogun shrines consist of heaps of scrap metal and are found both separately and as an essential part of altars dedicated to all other Edo deities. 'In every shrine Ogun is always first. It opens the way.' Yet Ogun also appears in the oral literature as a junior son of Osanobua sent out into the world with his cutlass to make farms and to make war. In this capacity, Ogun can be found portrayed in mud shrines either devoted to him or, more commonly, in shrines dedicated to his senior brother, Olokun (plate 50). In these he is always depicted in a red war costume carrying the tools and weapons of his varied occupations. Not only his costume but, significantly, his eyes are often painted red. To describe someone in Benin as having 'red eyes' is a way of indicating his violent temper and his capacity for causing harm. Ogun's dangerous power, however, can be used to protect his devotees, just as his sword can open the way to a better life.

Like Ogun in his abstract sense, Osun is not an anthropomorphic deity but a power which inheres in leaves and herbs collected in the forest. Specialists, called *ebo* in Edo, possess knowledge of the location of these ingredients and how to brew them into magical and medicinal preparations. Both Ogun and Osun, then, are concerned with the processing of raw materials and their transformation into instruments of power. While Ogun's powers are manifested on the physical level, in tools and weapons, those of Osun are psychic or spiritual. *Ebo* use their special knowledge to cure, to divine, to administer ordeals to suspected evildoers, and indeed to combat the greatest evil of all, the witches (plates 51 and 52).

The Edo believe that witches operate at night in the wild forest or bush. Their society is organized on hierarchical lines, with a king, chiefs, warriors, and magicians – a grisly parallel to the human world. At night witches meet in tree tops and send out their life force in the guise of a vicious night bird to take the life force of their intended victim and transform it into a passive animal like a goat or antelope, which they then devour. Because of his knowledge of the forest, the Osun specialist shares the same powers as the witch but uses them only for good ends.

One locus of the specialist's power is his iron staff, *osun ematon* (the iron *osun*). It is a long rod surmounted by a bird and decorated with figures of other birds, animals, reptiles, and a variety of objects of ritual and everyday use such as ceremonial swords and hoes (plate 54). The use of iron links the Osun specialist to the warrior, hunter, and craftsman, all of whom have Ogun as a patron deity. The staff itself represents flames shooting upward. Its praise name is *osun nigiogio*, the *osun* burning up with heat. The staff gives the specialist the power to escape danger and combat the evil world of the witches.[63]

Formerly the Benin pantheon was more complex but the worship of some deities, like Obiemwen, the great mother, seems to have fallen into abeyance. There are still numerous minor gods and goddesses: deified founders of ward guilds in Benin City; great war heroes, magicians, and faithful servants of past obas, particularly Ewuare and Ozolua; also worshipped are rebel warriors and fugitive queens who fled the court into the countryside and there transformed themselves into features of the environment: rivers, lakes, and hills.

Village Arts

The last two types of deities – the faithful and the rebellious – are the focus of rural cults found clustered throughout the kingdom, some in one village only, others in a group of contiguous villages, and still others spread over one of the large traditional subdivisions of the kingdom. These hero deities are worshipped by the community in order to ensure the health and well-being of all village members (plate 56).

There are certain art forms associated with these cults of hero deities. Each cult group has its own characteristic *ukhurhe*, a long segmented staff with a hollowed chamber just below the top in which a piece of wood is inserted to make a rattling sound when the staff is

53. *(Above)* **Obuobo's bell from the Village of Avbiama. Obuobo was the first** *Enogie* **(hereditary chief of the royal lineage) of Avbiama Village, a few miles from Benin City. The bell was kept in a special section of the village ancestral shrine. The imagery of this bell relates to the power of Osun (snakes issue from nostrils) and to the achievements of this legendary hero (the motif of the hand). Brass bells and other objects were once found scattered throughout the kingdom according to contemporary accounts, although it is not known whether they were created in the villages or sent from the capital. Styles often are so divergent from the royal brasswork that the former alternative must be considered.** 9¼in (23·5cm). *Lagos, Nigerian Museum*

54. *(Right)* **Iron Osun staff. The power of the Osun specialist resides in his staff, which enables him to transform into a bird or animal. The bird depicted on the top of this staff is** *akala,* **the grey heron, who is lord of the witches. Chameleons represent the power of transformation and are messengers in the night world.** 26½in (67cm). *Chicago, Field Museum of Natural History*

56. (*Above*) Ovbo cult dancer from Uzala Village

57. Igbile cult mask which is worn during the annual rituals of the Igbile cult in Ughoton Village, which was once the port of trade with Europeans, but may also have been a cultural contact point with other riveraine groups long before that time. The dancers sing in a language they identify as Ilaze (Ilaje Yoruba). It has been suggested that the masks show strong stylistic affinities to the art of the Niger Delta.[65]

55. (*Left*) *Ovia* rattle staff. The *ukhurhe* are the real symbols of Ovia.... They are massive staffs about four-and-a-half feet high, carved with representations of the *Ovia* masqueraders. More than anything else, they are identified with Ovia herself who is sometimes said to enter them when she is called upon by the priests.[64]

struck on the ground. This is the most widespread and, indeed, most basic form of all Benin cult objects (compare with the *Olokun* staff in plate 47 and the ancestral staff in plate 58). It is the top of the staff which generally designates the cult to which it belongs. The *Olokun ukhurhe*, as we have seen, represents a priest and an Olokun devotee, while the *Ovia ukhurhe* represents a masquerader (plate 55).

The rattle staff is both a means of communication with the spirit world, achieved when the staff is struck upon the ground, and a staff of authority, to be wielded only by the properly designated person. In this way, it is related to a variety of royal staffs of authority (see plate 70). Ideally, these cult staffs are obtained from the urban carvers' guild, *Igbesanmwan*, who are supposed to have a monopoly on their production, but in actuality local village age-grade members often produce them when needed for their own cults.

Most village cult shrines consist of these rattle staffs, pots with magical ingredients, and pieces of kaolin chalk. In some of them there are also mud figures similar in form to those found in Olokun shrines, discussed earlier. In fact, mud figures are mainly found in the shrines of river deities, such as Igbaghon, who are considered members of Olokun's court. Thus, they are never represented in the royal pose and regalia of kings, as in Olokun, but in the secondary but still imposing role of chiefs, queens, or powerful magicians.

There are a number of different village masking traditions. Whatever the cult, the mask wearers are usually called *erinmwi*, that is, representatives of the spirit world. The ceremonies in which they perform honour the hero deities as well as purify and protect the village from the evil forces that bring disease. For this reason the dancers' bodies are covered by a cloak of palm fronds, the smell of which is said to repel evil. In some cases, the palm fronds are overlaid with streamers of scarlet ceremonial cloth on which are sewn mirrors and brass cut-outs; again all these materials are supposed to repel evil. Wood is used to construct superstructures upon which are attached voluminous silk scarves, as in the *Okhuaihe* cult dance, or rows of red parrot feathers, used in the headdresses of *Ovbo ne Uzala* or *Ovia* dancers (plates 55, 56). Actual wooden masks are used in *Ekpo ne Igan* and *Ekoko ne Ute*, two village masking groups that come into Benin at the annual ceremony of *Igue* to entertain the crowds, as well as in two festivals of village cults which derive from other regions: *Igbile* of Ughoton Village (plate 57) based on Ilaje Yoruba and Ijo elements and *Eghughu* of Igue Osodin, derived from the Owo Yoruba *Egungun* masquerade.

The most widespread and best known cult with wooden masks is *Ekpo*, found mainly in the region of Iyekorhionmwon, an area to the south and east of the capital city, which long rebelled and fought

58. Three *ukhurhe* for ancestral altars. The one on the left, surmounted by a human head, represents generalized ancestors and is for a commoner's paternal ancestral altar. The one in the middle with an upraised thumb is for the nobility and is associated with the gesture of 'gathering up riches' found also on shrines of the Hand. The *ukhurhe* on the right is also reserved for the nobility and illustrates the proverb of ancestral power: 'The one who holds the fish can also let it loose'. *From left to right: 47½in (120cm); 52½in (133cm); 49½in (125·5cm). Chicago, Field Museum of Natural History*

against the central power. The founder of *Ekpo* cult was Agboghidi, a famous warrior who rebelled against Oba Akengbuda from his base in the village of Ugo in Iyekorhionmwon. From Ugo his warrior associates took the cult to other villages in that region. *Ekpo* cult is said to protect villagers from disease. At the annual dances, or whenever an epidemic threatens, the men of the middle age grade don masks representing a wide range of characters: Agboghidi the founder, Olokun, Osanobua, Igbaghon (plate 59) and other deities, court officials, sacrificial animals, famous Osun specialists, beautiful young women and men at the prime of life.[66]

Ekpo, *Ovia*, and *Okhuaihe*, as well as others of the masking cults, are associated with heroes or heroines who opposed the central government or deserted the oba. It is no wonder, then, that they are not allowed in Benin City. Should any mask or other cult object be brought into the capital, a special ceremony of purification must be performed.[67] Yet these cults are linked to the centre; all must announce their annual ceremonies to the king and receive his approval. And the *Ekpo* cult in particular establishes this link with the urban centre through its iconography. Masks are carved to represent not only the rebel hero who founded the *Ekpo* cult, but also to portray past chiefs, Osun specialists, and warriors, who mediated between the village and court and utilized their special powers on behalf of the king.

The Arts of Temporal Experience

Erinmwi, the world of the gods and hero deities, is ever present but invisible. It impinges on the everyday world as its denizens make demands and punish those who refuse to fulfill them. Sacrifice is man's way to appease these gods and request further favours. The relationship is contractual: in return for long life, health, and prosperity, man gives respect and gifts.

But there is also a temporal dimension to man's relationship with the spirit world. Each human soul must move between the two realms in a cycle of fourteen reincarnations. Before birth, a person comes before the creator god, Osanobua, and his senior son, Olokun, to inform them of his life's goals or destiny. This is not predestination in the Calvinist sense, since a person chooses his own fate, which is then confirmed by these two deities. The person's *ehi*, his alter-ego or 'guide' in the spirit world, stands beside him and thereafter keeps track of how well he has fulfilled the destiny that he has chosen. Intimately linked with individual destiny are the Benin notions about the mystical aspects of the human personality as embodied in the Head and the Hand.

The Head, according to Bradbury, 'symbolizes life and behaviour in this world, the capacity to organize one's actions in such a way as to

60. *(Above)* This *Ekpo* cult mask from Avbiama Village represents Chief Akpama who mediated between the villagers and the central authority. The mask is identified as a chief because of the semi-circular headdress, indicating the chiefly *akpata* haircut, and the row of coral beads worn only by the nobility

59. *(Left)* An *Ekpo* mask representing the goddess Igbaghon from the main shrine centre of her cult in the Iyekorhionmwon District. She is considered an extremely beautiful but temperamental deity, as is appropriate for the favourite wife of a polygamous monarch, Olokun, god of the waters

61. *(Left)* A shrine of the Hand in Benin City

62. *(Right)* Shrine of the Head in Benin City. The carved head rests on a special plate *(okpan)* with designs of kola nuts and sacrificial animals

survive and to prosper'.[68] Thus, it represents the individual who has not only chosen a fine destiny but has also accomplished all that he aimed at. Shrines to the Head are found in the most private chambers of chiefly homes. On the altar rests a carved wooden head, of exactly the same type as found on the ancestral altar, which is a direct representation of the successful life of the chief as expressed in his 'good head' (plate 62; compare with plate 66).

If someone has led a successful and prosperous life, he can then erect a shrine to his Hand, the representation of individual achievement in the worldly sense: the possession of slaves, wives, and animals. It is individual decision, not divine demand, that dictates when this altar will be erected; the person must feel he has indeed accomplished much in this world. The shrine of the Hand is generally carved in wood, although those apparently made for an eighteenth-century oba and *Ezomo* (plates 1, 34) were cast in brass. The shrine, called ikengobo, consists of two parts: a wooden cylinder on top upon which is carved the image of a successful warrior chief, and the rectangular or semi-circular base, with a frieze of sacrificial animals, representing all the creatures which the powerful chief has offered to the spirit world. The main image, of course, is a pair of hands with upraised thumbs, representing the gesture of 'gathering up riches into one's own hand' (plate 61).

When an individual has reached the end of his time on earth, successful or not, his body is buried and his soul returns to the spirit world to give an account of his life. His *ehi* must testify as well. Those who have lived well can hope to return again to the world of men, in many cases to their own families, to live out their cycle of fourteen reincarnations. Evildoers may be doomed to never return. On earth, the survivors perform an elaborate funeral ceremony to guide the soul to the spirit world and to ensure its incorporation as an ancestor. The senior son sets up an altar as the focal point for communication with his father; if a family altar already exists, he will simply add a carved rattle staff.

The art objects found on the Benin ancestral altar in large measure reflect the hierarchical social structure of the kingdom. The commoner's paternal ancestral altar is a rectangular platform. Resting upon the wall are wooden staffs, *urhurhe*, with a human head carved on the top of each of them (plate 58). If any predecessor of the present senior son had a title or was a well-known priest, his ceremonial sword, *ada*, might be found among the staffs. At least one rectangular bell is placed towards the front where it can be easily rung to announce the commencement of a service (plate 63). At the very front, the presence of a celt or 'thunderstone' signifies the sudden and dreadful power of Ogiuwu, the god of death.

63. Brass bell. Like the rattle staff, the bell on the ancestral altar is used to 'call the ancestors'. But this sort of bell also has warrior associations, for in the old days warriors used to wear such bells around their necks for protection in battle and to announce their victories on returning home (see plate 97). *Philadelphia, University of Pennsylvania Museum*

65. *(Above)* **Chief's ancestral altar, Benin City**

66. *(Above right)* **A wooden commemorative head. Chiefs who wish to decorate their ancestral altars can purchase heads such as this one. Although the local historian, Chief Egharevba, traces the origin of these to the Ogiso dynasty, members of the woodcarvers' guild disagree. According to Chief Ohanbamu Ineh, the form represents the head of Enekidi of Ogbelaka, a legendary figure said to have lived during the time of Oba Ozolua who was put to death after an unsuccessful rebellion. While the carving now has a purely decorative and commemorative function, this story alludes to the trophy head complex discussed earlier in plate 16**

The paternal ancestral altar of a chief has the same rectangular shape and contains the basic rattle staffs, bells, celts, and, of course, ceremonial swords as that of the commoner (plate 65). But the altar also contains objects forbidden to the commoner. A wooden commemorative head, of the same type as found on the shrine of the Head except that it does not rest on a special plate, is one of the main features of a noble's altar (plate 66). This head, called *uhunmwun-elao*, is considered by the Edo to be primarily decorative and not spiritually powerful. The altar is related to that of the Head in that it represents the proper and successful life of a chief who has now gone to reside in the spirit world. A special round stool, *erhe*, is placed directly in front of the altar for the use of the chief when he officiates as family priest (plate 64). The shape differs from the rectangular carved stool (see plate 10) used by chiefs as status symbols, but it is associated with the round white-washed mud seat, called by the same name, which is used by priests and priestesses of Olokun. The appearance of a stool so closely linked with the god of the waters evokes the image of the soul's voyage across the sea to the spirit world. Lastly, behind the altar is a long rectangular carved plank, called *urua*. This is found only on the shrines of very high ranking chiefs, and the sacrificial images carved on it allude to the powers these chiefs have over life and death.

The royal ancestral altar differs considerably from those of commoners or chiefs. It is round not rectangular in shape and is adorned with many objects not found on other types of altar (plate 68). Commemorative heads here, as on the chief's shrine, refer to the powers of the Head to direct life successfully. Those on the royal

64. *(Left)* **Wooden ancestral stool** *(erhe)*. **The images on it (frogs, mudfish and pythons) are all inhabitants of Olokun's realm. Benin City**

shrine, however, are made of brass not wood, a usage restricted to royalty (plate 69). Brass has a complex symbolic meaning in Benin. As a material that never corrodes or rusts, it stands for the permanence and continuity of kingship. Its shiny surface is considered beautiful, and in the past the royal brasses were constantly being polished to a high sheen. Lastly, brass is red in colour and this is considered by the Edo to be 'threatening', that is, to have the power to drive away evil forces. On the top of each head rests a carved ivory tusk. In the old days the king used to receive one tusk from every elephant killed in the kingdom; some were sold to European traders during the long years of commerce with the West, others were given as gifts to faithful chiefs, and still others were displayed on the royal ancestral shrines. Images on the tusks represent former kings, great war chiefs, soldiers, retainers, and animals symbolic of royal powers.

In the centre is a brass altarpiece (*aseberia*) representing the deceased king in full ceremonial regalia surrounded by his main courtiers and chiefs. He wears the coral bead outfit used only at *Igue* and *Ugie Erha Oba*, the two main ceremonies of divine kingship. In one hand he holds a ceremonial sword, *eben*, and in the other a proclamation staff (*isevbere-igho*) in the form of a gong (*egogo*). The small leopards on the sides represent large cast or carved leopards actually placed alongside the king in ceremonies (plate 67) and refer to the tamed leopards that once accompanied the king when he paraded in the city.

The Divine King

The ancestral altars are the major shrines in the palace. A king may have personal shrines to Olokun, his Hand, and so on, and there are a few royal gods, such as Uwen and Ora, but the altars honouring his ancestors are the only ones which are completely national in scope. The living monarch rules by virtue of being descended from Oranmiyan, the founder of this dynasty, and thus he is the caretaker of these shrines for the benefit of the Benin people. The king, like the commoner, officiates at the royal altars to request the aid of his ancestors, but, unlike the commoner, his predecessors are the protectors of the nation at large and their own divine power has passed on to him.

While the divinity of the oba indeed derives from his descent, it has wider moral sanctions. As the reigning monarch, he alone possesses the royal coral beads. Since other members of his immediate family can claim similar descent, possession of the beads and other royal relics determines who ultimately sits on the throne. This is made clear by the story related earlier about the conflict between the sixteenth-century king Esigie and his brother Aruaran, who battled for

67. A pair of brass or ivory leopards used to be placed at the side of the king when he sat in state, exactly as in the altarpiece in the previous plate. Each of the leopards shown here is made from five separate tusks. Their spots are copper discs and their eyes mirrors. It has been suggested that these are nineteenth-century copies of earlier models. [69] *32in (81·5cm). London, British Museum (on loan from H.M. the Queen)*

68 and 69. (*Right*) Royal ancestral altars in the palace, Benin City, with a detail showing one. Before 1897 there were individual altars for each deceased king, but there is now only one for each ruler since the reconstruction of the palace and a general altar for all the obas before 1897

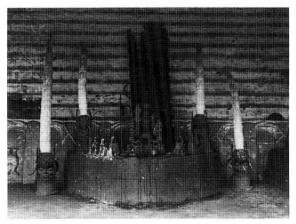

70. Figure of the oba in ceremonial dress.
This type of figure was placed on the royal
ancestral altar, the loop above, according to
Chief Ihama, enabling its easy removal for
polishing. In his right hand, the oba holds
an *eben*, a ceremonial sword with which he
dances to honour his ancestors, and in his
left hand he holds a proclamation staff,
isevbere igho, in the form of a gong, *egogo*.
There are both ivory and brass gongs. Some
are used as proclamation staffs and others,
particularly the ivory ones, used to drive
away evil forces in the Emobo ritual (see
plates 92 and 93). Eighteenth century.
*22½in (57·4cm). Fort Worth, Kimbell Art
Gallery*

71. Ivory figure of a king. This figure 'once stood on a post close to and in front of the King's house. It was collected by Dr Felix Norman Roth in 1897 when medical officer to the expedition to Benin and remained on clearing up after the forces had left.'[70]
15½in (39·5cm). Chicago, Field Museum of Natural History

possession of a special coral bead. The royal coral beads are not merely ornamental; they have the power of *ase*, that is, whatever is said with them will come to pass. The ability to curse and issue proclamations is one of the principal sanctions of the monarchy. As Chief Ihaza explained: 'The oba does not use Esigie's bead now because he does not swear or curse. If he swears or curses it would be impossible to revoke. Whatever he says will have effect.' The coral beads are not the only sources of the oba's power to curse: the proclamation staff, *isevbere-igho*, gives him the same power (plate 70) but the beads are probably more important for they define the monarchy and provide its mystical sanction. According to Chief Ihaza, 'When the king is wearing this heavy beaded costume, he does not shake or blink but stays still and unmoving. As soon as he sits down on the throne he is not a human being but a god.'

The oba was perhaps most godlike in one attribute: he alone had the right to take human life. In the court of law he was the final arbitrator of the death penalty, while in the course of ritual he alone offered human sacrifices (although a few of his most powerful chiefs were granted the same privilege). Thus 'attitudes towards the kingship were a complex of affection and awe, pride, and fear, but the overriding notion ... was one of fearfulness'.[71]

The position of the oba stems also from his cosmological status. As king of the dry land he is the counterpart of Olokun, king of the great waters. The wealth and power of the oba traces back to the time when Oba Ewuare went to the river and brought back the coral beads and other riches from Olokun's kingdom. Just as Olokun's palace is a source of beauty, wealth, and fecundity, so also is its earthly counterpart, the palace of the king of the dry land.

Art and Ritual in the Palace

The royal palace was considered the centre of the Benin world, and it is evident from travellers' reports how extensive and impressive a structure it was. Of far greater size and complexity than the compound of even the richest chief, it was also more highly decorated.

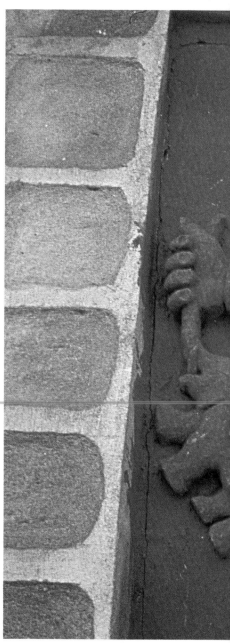

72. (*Above left*) **One of several entrances to the royal palace in Benin City. The moulded clay reliefs are now so worn that it is difficult to determine what they depict**

73. *(Above)* **Terracotta plaque on the side of the palace facing the street. A series of plaques, depicting famous obas, warriors and magicians, was commissioned by Oba Akenzua II from Ovia Idah, a traditional artist who incorporated long-established motifs into the new medium of terracotta. This plaque represents the coronation of Akenzua, when he sacrificed a leopard and an elephant**

In the accounts of members of the British Expedition we learn that the doors, lintels, and rafters of the council chamber and king's residence were lined with sheets of repoussé decorated brass covered with royal geometric designs and figures of men and leopards. Ornamental ivory locks sealed the doors and carved ivory figurines surmounted anterior posts (plate 71). A brass snake, observed for the first time by a European in the early eighteenth century, was still to be seen on the roof of the council chamber house.[72] Since its destruction in 1897, the palace has been rebuilt, although it is much reduced in size and splendour. Where once compounds existed for all the former kings, now only one large walled area encloses individual altars for each of the three immediate predecessors and one general altar for all the rest. Decorated sheets of brass, however, still adorn the rafters and lintels, and terracotta plaques now recount the exploits of former kings (plates 72 and 73).

The palace was, and still is to a certain extent, the focal point of Benin social aspirations. The accumulation of wealth is an avenue to high status, particularly when utilized in the purchase of a chiefly title in the palace. Each title is a political office but also a ritual responsibility. Indeed, most chiefs define their roles in terms of their ritual duties for the king.

The palace is the centre of ritual activity aimed at the well-being and prosperity of the Benin nation. Over and above domestic, guild, or village religious ceremonies, there is an annual cycle of rituals held within the confines of the palace. Some are of a private nature, such as the oba's sacrifices to his own *ehi*, *Ugie Ama*, or to his Hand, *Ihiekhu*. Others, to be described here, are public. In recent times, the number of public rituals performed has been reduced and their performance restricted to the Christmas vacation, but their meaning remains. These rituals draw upon a wide range of participants and demand enormous amounts of time and energy. Materials for use in the ceremonies, such as animals to be sacrificed or foodstuffs for offerings and gifts, come in from around the kingdom (plates 74 and 75). Some villages send groups of specialists to perform in specific ceremonies, such as the Ilobi villagers from Isi, specialists in the preparation of poisoned arrows, who come to participate in the *Isiokuo* mock war. Within the capital city, whole guilds are organized around their participation in ceremonies, among them drummers, shield bearers, ritual slaughterers and distributors of sacrificial animals. Craftsmen of all kinds, carvers, casters, weavers, leatherworkers and so on, provide regalia and ritual objects to be used in the ceremonies, while a vast number of Osun specialists work out intricate magical preparations. The various chiefly orders, the craftsmen, Osun specialists and others all have work and storage areas within the palace. It is a hub of activity; the Edo in fact draw the very apt parallel between the palace and the complex hierarchical organization and bustling activity of a large termite mound.

The king himself and his many chiefs have much to do to prepare themselves materially and spiritually for the ceremonies. Costumes must be made to order or refurbished, protective charms must be prepared and sacrifices performed to ensure success. In the Benin metaphor, 'going to a palace ceremony is like going to war'. Danger lurks from enemies of the king both within and outside the kingdom and one of the important duties of the chiefs is to provide magical

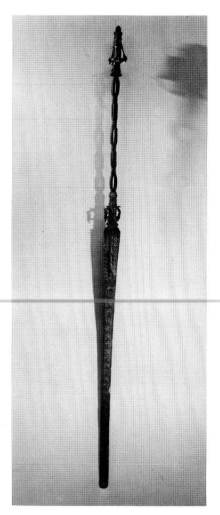

74. *(Above)* **Brass staff of office. A special group of buyers,** *Idemwin* **from the** *Ibiwe* **palace society, used to collect animals for sacrifice from villages. These brass swords were their staff of office. Other palace organizations, such as the carver's guild and traders (plate 24), had their own staffs of office.** *Philadelphia, University of Pennsylvania Museum*

75. *(Right)* **Brass plaque of cow sacrifice. Sacrifice is the focal point of nearly all Benin rituals. In former times the king used to sacrifice enormous numbers of animals, cattle being the highest form of domestic sacrifice offered.** *20in (51cm). London, British Museum*

77. *(Above)* High ranking chief dressed in an elaborate costume called 'pangolin skin'. Although made of imported red flannel, the material is cut in such a way as to imitate the skin of the pangolin, or scaly anteater, an animal which curls up when in danger and thus becomes invulnerable.

78. A brass ornament hanging down the back of the chiefly 'pangolin skin' outfit. It is called 'scorpion' (*Ekpakpahumwagan*). 'The brass scorpion worn ... by chiefs on their back is to indicate that the chief is as dangerous as a scorpion. ... In the olden days it was dangerous for a chief to be coming and going in the town. So he used to equip himself with such a charm.'[78]

76. *(Left)* Plaque of chiefs in pangolin costume. As comparison of this plaque with plate 77 demonstrates, there has been some continuity in ritual attire over the centuries and it may therefore be possible to reconstruct the background and meaning of many of the plaques. *18¼in (46·5cm). London, British Museum*

80. (*Above*) **Brass staff** (*ahianmwen-oro*). **At** *Ugie Oro* **chiefs carry this staff and hit the beak with a brass rod in remembrance of its ignominious prophecy.** *14in (35·5cm). New York, Metropolitan Museum*

79. (*Left*) **Brass hip ornaments** (*uhunmwun-ekhue*). **Chiefs of all ranks wear a brass mask on the left hip when dressed in full ceremonial regalia. In form it is related to the brass pendant masks sent to vassal rulers (plate 17) and the ivory pendant mask worn by the oba.** *Philadelphia. University of Pennsylvania Museum*

protection to augment the great mystical power of the oba himself (plates 76–79).

In former times, one chief, the *Aragwa*, was responsible for determining the dates of royal rituals through keeping track of the agricultural seasons and co-ordinating them with the specific days of the four-day Benin week considered appropriate for palace ceremonies.[74] The yearly round of rituals is grounded in the agricultural cycle – indeed it opens and closes with agricultural rites – but the ceremonies are primarily concerned with the purification and strengthening of the kingdom. Although not all are still performed, they will be described here in the order and form they once had.[75]

The festival of *Ikhurhe* opens the cycle. It takes place during the season of 'brushing the farm', that is, the period of preparation for planting when the ground is cleared and great trees are felled in the bush. This is approximately early March in our calendar. The purpose of *Ikhurhe* is to purify the land and ensure fertility for the crops soon to be planted. In every home offerings of snails and other 'cooling' materials are placed at the foot of the primordial *Ikhinmwi* tree, the shrine of the land, while various guilds perform a general purification for the land of the nation as a whole. Without the 'cooling' or ritual purification of the soil, no other palace event could take place.

Ikhurhe is followed by the Bead Festival (*Ugie Ivie*) and *Oro* Festival (*Ugie Oro*), both created by the sixteenth-century king Esigie in remembrance of his great internal and external wars. *Ugie Ivie* recalls the struggle between Esigie and his brother Aruaran of Udo over possession of the royal coral bead, which would be used to proclaim the capital of the kingdom. During the ceremony, all the beads of the kings, chiefs, and royal wives are gathered together on the palace altar in honour of King Ewuare, who first brought coral beads to Benin from the palace of Olokun, and the blood of a human sacrifice is poured over them (nowadays a cow is used). This blood gives mystical power to the beads and fortifies them for all following ceremonies. Thus, while *Ikhurhe* prepares and purifies the land of the kingdom at large, *Ugie Ivie* augments the power of the royal relics, the core of the monarchy. *Ugie Oro* follows. Every five days for the next three months, the king and chiefs dance in procession, outdoing themselves in lavishness of dress. It is considered so attractive a festival that, in the Benin adage, 'If a farmer participates in dancing *Oro* he will never take care of his farm.' As part of the ceremony, chiefs dance in a circle beating with a rod the beak of a cast brass bird in remembrance of the prophetic bird Esigie had killed on his way to success against the Igala people (plates 80 and 21). This commemorative element appears to have been grafted by Esigie on a basically ancestral rite started by an earlier king, Oba Ewedo, since throughout the period

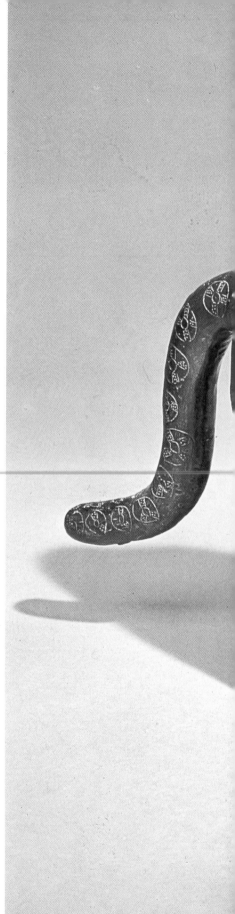

81. *(Above)* **Decorated vessel** *(igie)*. At *Ugie Erha Oba* the king taps the lid four times, accompanied by the prayer that he will sit firmly on the throne. 8¾in *(22cm)*. *Berlin, Museum für Völkerkunde*

82. *(Right)* **Plaque of two chiefs, possibly** *Ihama* **and** *Isekhurhe* **of** *Ihogbe*, **making offerings to the oba at** *Ugie Erha Oba*. 12½in *(32cm)*. *London, British Museum*

83. *(Far right)* **Brass aquamanile. After the oba finishes dressing and preparing himself for** *Ugie Erha Oba*, **he washes his hands with water from this leopard aquamanile. When not used in ceremony, the aquamanile rests on Oba Ewuare's altar.** *2in (30·5cm). London, British Museum*

sacrifices are made to the royal ancestors, a foreshadowing of the main ancestral rites to come.

Oba Esigie is said to have introduced the next two ceremonies as well, but with them the pendulum swings back from royal commemoration to general purification. The ritual of *Eghute* is aimed at the fertility of the nation, specifically formulated as an effort to prevent miscarriage and birth fatalities. All pregnant women are sent outside the city limits for the duration of the rites in order to protect them from the frightening secret activities. At the time of *Eghute*, 'messengers are sent to Prince Aruaran's gardens at Udo for a herb with which to make medicine that will cause corn and yam to fructify the same day as planted.'[76] Reiterating this theme, a chief (the title-holder *Osuan*) dressed as a pregnant woman, is said to magically conceive and deliver on the same day. At night he goes to the cemetery on Ikpoba hill, a place where witches congregate, and casts off his clothing, thus driving off the evil spirits that bring premature delivery and maternal death. Following *Eghute*, the *Orhu* festival is similarly supposed to repel evil. The high point of *Orhu* is the preparation by the oba's mother of a feast of pounded yam and soup without oil, which is taken

84. *(Above)* Wooden kola nut box with brass studs. Chiefs own elaborately carved boxes which they use for presenting gifts of kola nuts to the king at the Greetings Ceremony. This particular box represents an antelope or cow (interpretations differ), both of which are themselves used as offerings to the gods. 9½in (24·5cm). *Portland Art Museum*

85. *(Right)* This plaque represents the ceremonial official *Oton*. At *Ugie Erha Oba* and *Igue*, members of *Oton* carry whips with which they lash the air to drive away evil spirits. Under their robes they wear the jaw bone of deceased Town Chiefs. When a Town Chief died, the oba claimed his lower jaw, 'the jaw he used to dispute with the oba', symbolizing the ultimate supremacy of the king over his people. *Probably sixteenth century. 18in (45·5cm). London, British Museum*

86. (*Left*) Ivory mask probably worn at the hip by the oba as part of his costume for *Ugie Iye Oba*, the commemorative rites for his deceased mother. The late Oba Akenzua II identified this mask as representing Idia, the mother of King Esigie, because of the Portuguese heads round the top. Esigie is said to have been the oba reigning when the Portuguese first arrived in Benin. Just as 'three' is the number of superorbital marks associated with Benin males, so 'four' is associated with Benin females.[77] 9⅞in (25cm). *London, British Museum*

87. (*Above*) **Members of the** *Ikpe-iwini* **subsection of the** *Ogbelaka* **guild.** 17½in (44·5cm). *London, British Museum*

by the palace group *Irho-Ema* and placed at all nine gates to the city as an offering to keep away evil forces. These gates are considered to be crossroads, and all crossroads are viewed by the Edo as the meeting point of the spirit world and the world of every day life, and so are the focus of offerings made to potentially harmful spirits. *Orhu* is said to have been introduced by Oba Esigie to commemorate a feast prepared by his mother Queen Idia before he left for the Udo war.[78]

All these rituals are building up towards the two most important rites of the year: *Ugie Erha Oba*, which honours the king's deceased father, and *Igue* which strengthens his own mystical powers. Both ceremonies are said to have been instituted by Oba Ewuare. *Ugie Erha Oba* and *Igue* are paired conceptually in that both are of paramount importance and have a tripartite structure. They differ, as Oba Akenzua II himself pointed out, in that in *Ugie Erha Oba* the king is the officiator while in *Igue* he is the object.[79] *Ugie Erha Oba* is the culmination of a series of ancestral rites. As a prelude, all families in Benin celebrate *Eho* for their own paternal ancestors. This general service is followed by palace rites (*Ugie Igun*) honouring each former king individually, ending at *Ugie Erha Oba* with the immediate predecessor of the present king. The ritual is full of the symbolism of royal supremacy. It opens with the Greeting Ceremony, *Otue*, in which the oba, seated before his father's altar, accepts the homage of the chiefs, as one by one in order of seniority they come to greet him,

88. (*Above*) **The drummers who appear in this photograph, and in the plaque in plate 87, are a subsection** (*Ikpe-iwini*) **of the** *Ogbelaka* **guild. This guild has important duties at the investiture of chiefs and in palace rituals such as** *Igue*. **The** *Ikpe-iwini* **subsection play the drums and** *Eneha* **sing songs in a secret language, unknown even to other guild subsections.**

89. (*Right*) **Oba Akenzua II in full coral bead regalia**

90 and 91. As *Igue* draws to an end, the *Uwangue* brings the oba a ceremonial box, *ekpokin*, with gifts from the king of Ife, 'his father'. This type of box, shown both in the photograph to the left and the plaque to the right, was made by the leather workers' guild in Benin for ceremonial gifts. Similar types are also found among the southern and eastern Yoruba and Igala. *Plaque: 21¼in (54cm). Berlin, Museum für Völkerkunde*

and in return, he makes them gifts of kola nuts and wine (plates 84 and 86). Their acceptance of these gifts, indeed their very participation in the ceremony, is an acknowledgement of the hierarchical political structure and the supremacy of the king. The main ceremony of *Ugie Erha Oba* is a lavish affair. Chiefs wear their most expensive costumes and dance with a ceremonial sword, *eben*, each trying to outdo the others in elegance and grace. The king wears his most elaborate beaded outfit and he, too, dances with an *eben* – the highlight of the ceremony – before his father's altar. Many sacrifices are offered to avert evil spirits, to appease the earth, and especially to honour and propitiate the oba's late father. On the third day a mock war, *Iron*, is staged against the Seven *Uzama* who are vanquished by the supporters of the king, just as all other foes during the year to come will be vanquished (plates 81–83).

Igue is also divided into three parts, beginning with a Greeting Ceremony, but its focus is more on a spiritual level. The main rite, *Igue* itself, centres around the oba's mystical powers. Roots, herbs, and seeds, the 'life-giving products of the forest', are made into a magical

92 and 93. *(Above and left)* **The oba at the** *Emobo* **ceremony strikes an ivory gong to drive away evil forces. Similar rituals are carried out in the villages when supernatural danger threatens. Outside the palace, however, iron gongs are used. The royal gong (left) is made of ivory (white being a symbol of ritual purity) and has carved designs of crocodiles, mudfish, water tortoises and snakes – all drawn from Olokun's pure and perfect world. The predominance of allusions to ritual purity reflects the ideal state to which** *Emobo* **aims.** *Gong: 14¼in (36cm). London, British Museum*

94. *(Right)* **Elaborately carved ivory bracelets such as these were the prerogative of the oba. According to Chief Ovbiebo of the** *Enisen* **section of** *Iwebo* **palace society, the group assigned the selection and co-ordination of the oba's ceremonial wardrobe, ivory bracelets are worn especially in ceremonies in which the oba dances with the** *eben* **sword or handles a gong, because they keep his coral beads from getting tangled.** *5¼in (13cm). London, British Museum*

potion that is applied to the different parts of the oba's body by *Ogiefa*, the priest responsible for the purification of the earth, and the *Ihama* of *Ihogbe*, the representative of the oba's family. All the animals of royal symbolic significance – the leopard, king of the bush animals, the vulturine fish eagle, king of the day birds, as well as the usual cows and goats – are sacrificed to the oba's Head, the locus of his wisdom and capacity to succeed. With the oba's well-being is identified the well-being of the nation and by this rite ... the welfare of the oba and his people is ensured for another year.'[80]

On the last day, children rush from their homes early in the morning carrying torches to drive away evil spirits. Once outside the

95. Plaque of *Amufi* acrobats. The *Amufi* dance is performed in a cotton tree. The night before the performance the ropes are secretly arranged in the tree so that the acrobats can appear to fly. *17in (43cm). Lagos, National Museum*

96. Plaque of oba with two chiefs at *Ague* **ceremony. The costumes in this plaque are identified as those worn by the king and his two titleholders, Chiefs** *Osa* **and** *Osuan,* **at** *Ague.* **Although of similar form, the oba's hat is made of beads while that of** *Osa* **and** *Osuan* **are of raffia palm. Because of this fabric and the secrecy of the** *Ague* **ceremony, there is a proverb that 'it is only Osa and Osuan that know what is in the palm frond'.** *Probably sixteenth century. London, British Museum*

town they gather up *ewere* leaves, called 'leaves of joy' and bring them home as signs of hope and happiness. In a similar vein, chiefs bring *ewere* leaves to the palace as a sign that *Igue* has gone well and that the oba and his people will prosper in the coming year (plates 87–91).

Once the oba's powers have been fortified, he utilizes them in ceremonies to purify and strengthen the nation. The festival of *Emobo* follows *Igue*. It differs from earlier rites in that there are no sacrifices, elaborate chiefly dances, or ceremonial appearances by the oba's wives and children. Its sole purpose is to drive away any evil forces that have somehow remained despite the previous ceremonies. To this end, the oba sits in a specially constructed pavilion made of red

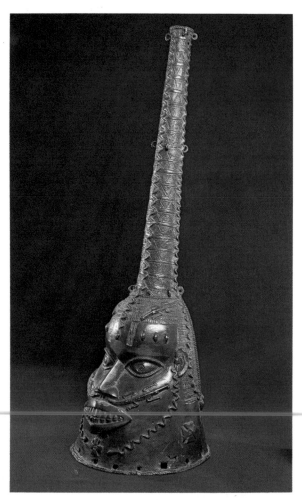

97. *(Above left)* A plaque of a chief wearing the ceremonial war dress *(akpa)* for *Isiokuo.* Around his neck hangs a bell for protection and signalling victory. The face of the leopard decorating the cloth (see plate 99, left) is to strike fear into the hearts of the enemy. The leopards' teeth necklace has a similar protective meaning. A red parrot feather assures him of success and a horsetail hanging from the helmet is a mark of prestige. In one hand he holds a spear *(ogala)*, in the other a shield *(asa)*. Accompanying him are two horn players. *22¼in (56·5cm). London, British Museum*

98. *(Above)* An Ododua mask, representing the great Osun specialist Ora who accompanied Oranmiyan from Ife. *22in (56cm). London, British Museum*

99. *(Left)* Warrior's costume (see plate 97). *22in (56cm). London, British Museum*

100. *(Right)* An Ododua mask representing Uwen (see plate 101). *London, British Museum*

101. Ododua ceremony. There are seven dancers in the Ododua performance representing two great Osun specialists, Uwen and Ora, and their entourage who accompanied Oranmiyan from Ife. The masks in the photograph are contemporary, made after 1897 while the two in the Museum of Mankind (plates 98 and 100) date to the eighteenth-century reign of Oba Eresonyen, who is said to have introduced this masquerade

cloth – red being a 'threatening' colour, one with the capacity to drive away evil. Later he dances with an ivory gong, striking it to repel malevolent spirits (plates 92–94). The ritual ends with Chief Esogban calling out: 'Any spirits that have not received offerings should go to Udo and eat', thus driving the last remnants of evil to the ancient rival town of Udo.

The simile that 'going to a palace ceremony is like going to war' is almost literally true in *Isiokuo*, a ceremony in honour of Ogun, god of iron and of war (plate 95). Dressed in military regalia, the oba and chiefs parade from the palace to the shrine of the God of War and there watch the *Amufi* acrobats display their skills in the high cotton tree, whirling and turning in what is described as a war against the sky (plate 95).

The yearly cycle ends as it began, with an agricultural rite, but one with wider implications. From the start of the New Yam Festival, *Ague*, until it is over, it is forbidden to consume or offer to the gods newly harvested yams. *Ague* is held in extreme secrecy within a special room in the palace and only the oba and a few members of *Ogbelaka* guild know what happens inside (plate 96). Oba Eresonyen added a subsidiary festival to *Ague* called *Ague Osa* (*Ague* of the Supreme God). *Ague Osa* honours the progenitor of the royal lineage, Ododua, the father of Oranmiyan. The officiators are the chiefly titleholders *Osa* and *Osuan*, who are the caretakers of the royal gods Uwen and Ora, a deified Osun specialist and his wife who are said to have come from Ife with Oranmiyan. The dance of *Ododua* is performed by seven masqueraders who wear brass helmet masks and hold ceremonial swords. They dance back and forth before the oba seven times, a sign of their loyalty and commitment to his protection (plates 98, 100, 101).

With *Ague*, the cycle has come full circle. All that has been harvested during the year may be consumed, evil forces have repeatedly been driven from the land, and the oba is strengthened and ritually fortified for the coming year. As the Edo say, 'Everything is cool.'

In recent years the annual ritual cycle has been curtailed, and the creation of art objects and costumes for these ceremonies, as well as for other religious and prestige activities, has diminished. Yet this hardly marks the end of Benin art. It has shown over the centuries a remarkable resilience in the face of all kinds of change, whether political, economic, social or religious. Today traditional forms, such as mud shrine figures and ancestral altar furnishings continue to be made, and new forms are emerging from the traditional base to become an integral part of modern Benin culture.

Bibliography

Abbass, Donna Kathleen: *European Hats Appearing in Benin Art*. M.A. Thesis, Department of Anthropology, Southern Illinois University, 1972

Alagoa, E. J.: 'The Niger Delta States and Their Neighbors 1600–1800', in *History of West Africa* (eds. J. F. A. Ajayi and Michael Crowder). Vol. I, 2nd edition. Columbia University Press, New York, 1976

Allmann, R.: 'With the Punitive Expedition to Benin City', *The Lancet* (London), II, July 3, 1898, pp. 43–4

Ben-Amos, Dan: *Ake Cult and Culture*, n.d., unpublished ms.

Ben-Amos, Paula: 'Men and Animals in Benin Art', *Man*, N.S., II, 2, 1976, pp. 243–52

Ben-Amos, Paula: 'Owina N'Ido: Royal Weavers of Benin', *African Arts*, XI, 4, 1978, pp. 49–53

Ben-Amos, Paula: 'Symbolism in Olokun Mud Art', *African Arts*, VI, 4, 1973, pp. 28–31, 95

Ben-Amos, Paula and Osarenren Omoregie: 'Keeping the Town Healthy: Ekpo Ritual in Avbiama Village', *African Arts*, 1969, II, 4, pp. 8–13, 79

Boston, J.: 'Notes on the Origin of Igala Kingship', *Journal of the Historical Society of Nigeria*, 2, December 1962, pp. 373–83

Boston, J.: 'Oral Traditions and the History of the Igala', *Journal of African History*, X, 1, 1969, pp. 29–43

Bradbury, R. E.: *Benin Studies* (ed. Peter Morton-Williams). Oxford University Press, London, 1973

Bradbury, R. E.: 'Divine Kingship in Benin', *Nigeria*, 62, 1959, pp. 186–207

Bradbury, R. E.: Notes on file at University of Birmingham Library.
   A series: Field notes, Benin City and surroundings, 1951/52
   B series: Notes on 35mm Film Series, 1958
   BS series: Benin Scheme Field notes, 1957–61
   R series: Files, n.d.

Bradbury, R. E.: *The Benin Kingdom and the Edo-Speaking Peoples of South-Western Nigeria*. International African Institute, London, 1957

[Burton, Sir Richard] 'An F.R.G.S.': 'My Wanderings in West Africa: A Visit to the Renowned Cities of Wari and Benin', *Fraser's Magazine*, LXVII, 1863, February, March, April, pp. 135–57, 273–89, 407–22

Clifford, Miles: 'A Nigerian Chiefdom. Some Notes on the Igala Tribe in Nigeria and Their "Divine-King"', *J.R.A.I.* LXVI, 1936, p. 424

Connah, Graham: 'How Archaeology can Supplement History: The Example of Benin', in *Discovering Nigeria's Past* (ed. T. Shaw). Oxford University Press, Ibadan, 1975(a)

Connah, Graham: *The Archaeology of Benin*. Clarendon Press, Oxford, 1975(b)

Cordwell, J. M.: *Some Aesthetic Aspects of Yoruba and Benin Cultures*. Ph.D. Thesis, Department of Anthropology, Northwestern University, 1952

Dark, Philip J. C.: *An Introduction to Benin Art and Technology*. Clarendon Press, Oxford, 1973

Dark, Philip: *Benin Art*. Paul Hamlyn, London, 1969

Dark, Philip J. C.: 'Benin Bronze heads: Styles and Chronology', in *African Images: Essays in African Iconology* (eds. Daniel F. McCall and Edna G. Bay). Africana Publishing Co., New York, 1975

Dark, Philip J. C.: *The Art of Benin: A Catalogue of an Exhibition of the A. W.F. Fuller and Chicago Natural History Museum*. Chicago, 1962

Darling, Patrick: 'The Elephant hunters, Slave Trade and Old Canoe-Port of Benin', unpublished ms., 1978

Dike, K. O.: 'Benin: A Great Forest Kingdom of Medieval Nigeria', *The UNESCO Courier*, No. 10, October, 1959, pp. 12–14

Egharevba, Jacob U.: *Benin Law and Custom*. 3rd edition. C. M. S. Niger Press, Port Harcourt, Nigeria, 1949

Egharevba, Jacob U.: *Short History of Benin*. 4th edition. Ibadan University Press, 1968 (1934)

Fagg, Bernard and William Fagg: 'The Ritual Stools of Ancient Ife', *Man*, No. 155, August, 1960, pp. 113–155

Fagg, William: *Afro-Portuguese Ivories*. Batchworth Press, London, 1959

Fagg, William: *Christie's: Tribal Art. Wednesday, July 13, 1977*, pp. 32–33

Fagg, William: *Christie's: Important Tribal Art. Tuesday, June 13, 1978*, pp. 42–45

Fagg, William: *Nigerian Images*. Percy Lund, Humphries & Co. Ltd., London, 1963

Fraser, Douglas: *Village Planning in the Primitive World*, London, 1968

Garlake, P.: 'Excavations at Obalara's Land, Ife, Nigeria', *West African Journal of Archaeology*, 4, 1974, pp. 111–148

Henderson, Richard N.: *The King in Every Man: Evolutionary Trends in Onitsha Ibo Society and Culture*. Yale University Press, New Haven, 1972

Herbert, Eugenia W.: 'Aspects of the Use of Copper in Pre-Colonial West Africa', *Journal of African History*, XIV, 2, 1973, pp. 179–194

Hodgkin, T. (ed.): *Nigerian Perspectives: An Historical Anthology*. London, 1960

Johnson, Marion: 'The Cowrie Currencies of West Africa: Part I', *Journal of African History*, XI, 1, 1970, pp. 17–49

Jungwirth, Mechthildis: *Benin in den Jahren 1485–1700*. Verlag Notring, Wien, 1968

Landolphe, Capitaine: *Memoires du Capitaine Landolphe, contenant l'histoire de ses voyages pendant trent-dix ans aux côtes d'Afriques et aux deux Amériques* (ed. J. S. Quesne). Arthus Bertrand, Paris, 1823

Ling Roth, H.: *Great Benin: Its Customs, Art and Horrors*. Routledge & Kegan Paul Ltd., London, 1968 (1903)

Lopasic, Alexander: 'The "Bini" Pantheon Seen Through the Masks of the "Ekpo" Cult', *Reincarnation et vie mystique en Afrique Noire; Colloque de Strasbourg 16–18 mai, 1963*. Presses Universitaires de France, Paris, 1965

Marshall, H. F.: *Intelligence Report on Benin City*. Unpublished report in The Ministry of Local Government, Benin City, 1939

Melzian, Hans: *A Concise Dictionary of the Bini Language of Southern Nigeria*. Kegan Paul, Trench, Trubner & Co., Ltd., London, 1937

Murray, K. C.: *Catalogue of Exhibits in The Benin Museum Transferred From the Custody of the Benin Divisional Council to the Federal Department of Antiques on 26th August, 1960*, [found in Bradbury, Notes R67 Benin Art]

Nigerian Observer, IX, No. 2452, Monday, November 15, 1976, p. 1.

Obayemi, Ade: 'The Yoruba and Edo-Speaking Peoples and their Neighbors before 1600', in *History of West Africa* (eds. J. F. A. Ajayi and Michael Crowder). Vol. I, 2nd edition. Columbia University Press, New York, 1976

Read, C. H. and O. M. Dalton: *Antiquities of the City of Benin and from Other Parts of West Africa in the British Museum*. William Clowes & Sons, Ltd., London, 1899

Royal Gold Coast Gazette, No. 21, Vol. 1, Tuesday, March 25, 1823, pp. 73–74

Ryder, A. F. C.: *Benin and the Europeans 1485–1897*. Longmans, Green and Co., Ltd., London, 1969

Shaw, Thurston: *Nigeria: Its Archaeology and Early History*. Thames and Hudson, London, 1978

Shaw, T.: 'Spectographic Analyses of the Igbo and other Nigerian Bronzes', *Archaeometry*, 8, 1965, pp. 86–95

Sheldon, Kathleen: 'An Examination of Bini-Portuguese Ivory Saltcellers'. Unpublished paper, Art History Department, Columbia University, 1977

Struck, B.: 'Chronologie der Benin Altertümer', *Zeitschrift für Ethnologie*, LV, 1923, pp. 113–166.

Tahal (Water Planning) Ltd.: *Master Plan For Urban and Rural Water Supply*. (Report submitted to the Ministry of Works and Transport, Mid-Western Nigeria.) Tel-Aviv, 1965

Talbot, P. Amaury: *The Peoples of Southern Nigeria*, II. Frank Cass & Co., Ltd., London, 1969 (1926)

Umberger, Emily: 'Benin-Style Bronze Masks'. Unpublished paper, Art History Department, Columbia University, 1978

Van Nyandael, David: 'A Description of Rio Formosa, or, The River of Benin', in *A New and Accurate Description of the Coast of Guinea* (ed. William Bosman). J. Knapton, London, 1705

Von Luschan, F.: *Die Altertümer von Benin* (3 vols.). Museum für Völkerkunde, Berlin, 1919

Werner, O.: 'Metallurgische Untersuchungen der Benin-Bronzen des Museums für Völkerkunde, Berlin', *Baessler-Archiv*, N.F. XVIII, 1, 1970, pp. 71–153

Willett, Frank: *African Art, an Introduction*. Thames and Hudson, London, 1967

Willett, F.: 'Archaeology', in *Sources of Yoruba History* (ed. S. O. Biobaku). Clarendon Press, Oxford, 1973(a)

Willett, Frank: *Ife in the History of West African Sculpture*. Thames and Hudson, London, 1967

Willett, Frank: 'The Benin Museum Collection', *African Arts*, XI, 4, 1973(b), pp. 8–17